Lernkrimi Englisch

A Cry in the Darkness

Oliver Astley
Caroline Simpson

Vokabeltraining
zum Buch!

Lerne die Vokabeln zu diesem Buch: Mit phase6,
Deutschlands führenden Vokabeltrainer.

Mit phase6 übst du deine Vokabeln über Computer,
Tablet und Smartphone mit Android oder iOS.

**Der Circon Verlag schenkt dir die erste
Vokabelsammlung zu seinen Büchern.
Nur erhältlich über diesen Link (QR-Code).**

www.phase6.de/s/a2761

   Der beste Sprachtrainer für die Schule.

© Circon Verlag GmbH
Baierbrunner Straße 27, 81379 München
Ausgabe 2024
6. Auflage

Alle Rechte vorbehalten. Nachdruck, auch auszugsweise,
nur mit ausdrücklicher Genehmigung des Verlages gestattet.

Redaktion: Sigrid Oser
Fachkorrektur: Gina Billy
Produktion: Ute Hausleiter
Titelillustration: Karl Knospe
Lernkrimi-Logo: Carsten Abelbeck
Gestaltung: EKH Werbeagentur, textum GmbH
Umschlaggestaltung: red.sign GbR, Stuttgart

ISBN: 978-3-8174-1974-6
381741974/6

Besuchen Sie uns auf Instagram und Facebook: circonverlag

www.circonverlag.de

Vorwort

Liebe Leserin, lieber Leser,

sicher zum Lernerfolg – mit Spaß und Spannung! Die Compact Lernkrimis mit ihrer Kombination aus Lektüre und didaktischem Übungsanteil eignen sich hervorragend, um breite Sprachkompetenzen in der Fremdsprache zu erwerben. Der Lerner wird dabei durch die spannende Handlung, das angemessene Sprachniveau und den stetig ansteigenden Schwierigkeitsgrad der Übungen gefördert und motiviert.
Entwickelt nach neuesten Erkenntnissen der Fremdsprachendidaktik, sind Compact Lernkrimis das ideale Medium für einen Lernerfolg im Selbststudium. Durch die kleinen Texteinheiten und den hohen Übungsanteil sind sie aber auch als Unterrichtslektüre bestens geeignet.

So lernen Sie mit Compact Lernkrimis:
- **Mit Begeisterung lernen:** Die packende Krimihandlung motiviert Sie beim Lesen des englischen Originaltextes.
- **Wissen intensivieren und erweitern:** Durch die Kombination aus didaktisch aufbereiteter Lektüre und textbezogenen Übungen testen und trainieren Sie Ihre Sprachkenntnisse effektiv. Vokabelangaben auf jeder Seite unterstützen Sie beim Lesen.
- **Systematisch lernen:** Knüpfen Sie an Ihr individuelles Sprachniveau an und setzen Sie sich eigene Lernziele.
- **Unabhängig sein:** Lernen Sie individuell – wo und wann immer Sie wollen.

Viel Spaß beim **spannenden Erlernen der englischen Sprache**
wünscht Ihnen

Prof. Dr. Christiane Neveling
Didaktik der romanischen Sprachen, Universität Leipzig

Inhalt

A Cry in the Darkness 5

Death at the Lake 35

Deadly Duet 67

Final Test 101

Answers 105

Glossary 109

List of Exercises 122

Die Ereignisse und die handelnden Personen in diesem Buch sind frei erfunden. Etwaige Ähnlichkeiten mit tatsächlichen Ereignissen oder lebenden Personen wären rein zufällig und unbeabsichtigt.

A Cry in the Darkness

Oliver Astley

 A Cry in the Darkness

"Charlie! Charlie! Where are you?"

Janet Drummond is alone in the woods. She shines her torch into the trees, but she cannot see anything. She stops and listens.

She can only hear the sea forty metres below. The rhythmic sound of the water is almost hypnotic. There is not much wind tonight, but the summer air is cold. Long, black clouds are moving slowly past the full moon.

Janet starts walking again. Where is Charlie?

woods	Wäldchen
to shine a torch	mit einer Taschenlampe leuchten
almost	fast
past	*hier:* vorbei (an)
shouting	Geschrei
beer can	Bierdose

She hears shouting from somewhere. It must be those teenagers, she thinks. They always meet near the beach in the evening – and they leave their empty beer cans and cigarette packets! No respect…

"Charlie! Come to Mummy!"

The shouting is louder now. There are three people shouting, maybe four. And one of them is definitely a girl. Janet can't hear exactly what they're saying.

> Zu vielen deutschen Adjektiven auf *-isch* gibt es eine englische Entsprechung, die auf *-ic (hypnotic, ironic, rhythmic)* oder *-ical (political, typical)* endet.

A thick cloud covers the moon. It is now very dark, and Janet begins to feel a little nervous. She walks through the woods almost every night. But normally, Charlie is with her.

suddenly	plötzlich
cry	Schrei
fence	Zaun
cliff	Klippe
frightened	verängstigt
noise	Geräusch
glove	Handschuh

A minute later, she walks out of the trees and sits down at a picnic table. They are for the many tourists who come to Lynton on holiday. There is a car park for the tourists, too. Most nights the car park is empty. But tonight, there is an old caravan and two cars.

Janet is from the village of Lynton. Today, it is a very different place, she thinks. More people, more hotels and restaurants…

Suddenly, there is a loud cry in the darkness. Some birds fly into the air.

"Get your hands *off* me!" It is the same girl again. The words are far away, but very clear.

Janet stands up and walks to the fence by the cliff. She wants to see what is happening. Is the girl angry or frightened?

Just then, a noise comes from the trees on the other side of the car park.

"Charlie! There you are!"

The brown spaniel runs happily towards the fence. He has an old glove in his mouth.

"What is it, boy? Where were you? I think it's time to go home!" Janet tells her dog.

She walks through the car park to take the road back to the village. A black and yellow bike is lying on the ground next to the caravan.

That's young Ryan Weston's bike, thinks Janet. He's always **up to no good**!

Exercise 1: True or false? Welche Aussagungen sind korrekt? Markieren Sie mit richtig ✔ oder falsch – !

1. It is a warm summer night.
2. Charlie is not frightened.
3. Janet cannot see people in the woods.
4. Ryan Weston is a good boy.
5. There is no fence by the cliff.

Early the next morning, Sophie and Lukas Gruber are walking hand in hand along the beach. The sun is dancing on the water and the cool, fresh air is wonderful.

"This is so pretty!" says Lukas. "I love the sea. It's the only thing that Austria doesn't have."

Sophie laughs. Her Austrian **husband** is so patriotic.

"It's such a lovely **view**," says Lukas. "And the village is so high up! I can understand why people call it 'Little Switzerland'… What?"

to be up to no good	nichts Gutes im Schilde führen
husband	Ehemann
view	Ausblick, Aussicht
tight	*hier*: fest

Sophie is now holding his hand very **tight**. She is looking towards the cliff.

"What is it?" asks Lukas.

"What's that over there? Can you see? It looks like…"

About fifty metres away, something black is lying on the rocks. A dark object with… two red boots?

about	*hier*: circa
rubbish	Abfälle
wife	Ehefrau
Detective Chief Inspector (DCI)	Hauptkommissar
body	*hier*: Leiche

Sophie quickly walks to the bottom of the cliff. Lukas stays where he is.

"It's just **rubbish** from the sea," he calls out. "Look, there must be twenty beer cans between us!"

"Oh my god!" shouts Sophie. "Come here!"

Lukas runs to his **wife** and opens his eyes wide in shock.

> Spontane Entscheidungen drückt man im Englischen wie hier mit dem Futur aus. Man sagt also nicht: "I call the police."

The black object is not rubbish, but a designer coat. There is a person inside – a young woman with light blonde hair. Her skin is blue. She is definitely dead.

"Don't touch her!" says Lukas. "I'll call[i] the police."

Sophie looks up into the sky. "The poor woman," she says slowly. "It's such a long way to fall."

Exercise 2: Choose the correct alternative. Lesen Sie weiter und wählen Sie die richtige Variante!

At half past eight **1.** on / at Saturday morning, **Detective Chief Inspector** Lloyd is at the beach. He **2.** stands / is standing by the **body** with a police officer in uniform and two specialists in white clothes. They 3. are taking / is taking a lot of photographs. There 4. is / are more officers and an ambulance in the car park at the top of the 5. clipp / cliff. Blue lights are flashing.

The journalist Frank Thomson is at the beach with some other people from Lynton. They are trying to see what is happening.

"Who is it, Inspector?" shouts Frank. "What can you tell us?"
"It looks like suicide to me," says an old man to his left.
"I think so, too," says a woman

ambulance	Krankenwagen
to flash	blinken
suicide	Selbstmord
to remember	sich erinnern
locals *pl*	Einheimische

to his right. "Do you remember that suicide in 1977? A young man…very tragic!"
The inspector slowly walks up to the group of locals. He moves elegantly across the rocks for a man in his fifties. His white hair and beard are shining in the sun.
"You can all go home. There's nothing to see," he says.
"Do you know who it is?" asks Frank.
"I can't tell you anything at the moment, Mr Thomson," Inspector Lloyd explains. "It's very early for you to be at work, isn't it?"
"No, Inspector. I live here in the village. I saw all the lights from my bedroom window."

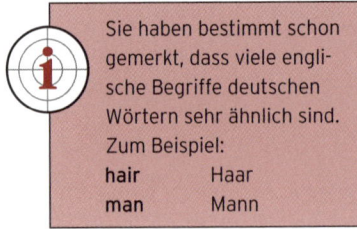

Sie haben bestimmt schon gemerkt, dass viele englische Begriffe deutschen Wörtern sehr ähnlich sind.
Zum Beispiel:
hair Haar
man Mann

to report	berichten
to reply	antworten
step	Schritt
bark	Gebell

"Oh? So you don't live in Barnstaple any more?"

Barnstaple is the nearest large town in North Devon,[i] a green and quiet part of South West England. The journalist and the inspector often meet each other when there is news to report.

"No," replies Frank. "I live here with my girlfriend now."

"Ah, one step closer to becoming husband and wife!" the inspector smiles.

At that moment, a long, loud bark fills the air. Everyone turns to look.

> Die Grafschaft **Devon** im Südwesten Englands grenzt an Cornwall. Lynton liegt an der Nordküste Devons und ist Teil des Exmoor Nationalparks, in dem man neben spektakulären Klippen und schönen Stränden auch einsame Moore und grüne Flusstäler entdecken kann.

Janet Drummond is talking to Sophie and Lukas Gruber. Beside her, Charlie the spaniel cannot keep quiet. It looks like he is trying to run towards the inspector.

Exercise 3: Match up the words. Welche Wortpaare gehören zusammen? Ordnen Sie zu!

1. ☐ village   a) bark
2. ☐ sea   b) shines
3. ☐ torch   c) wife
4. ☐ dog   d) locals
5. ☐ husband   e) beach

 The Mystery Woman

That afternoon, Janet Drummond is in the village shop. She is buying some bread and two cans of dog food.

"That's three pounds fifty-five, please," says the shop assistant. She is not very friendly today.

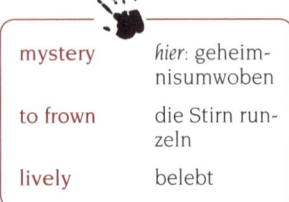	
mystery	*hier*: geheimnisumwoben
to frown	die Stirn runzeln
lively	belebt

"Are you okay, Abi?" Janet asks.

"I'm fine, sorry, just a bit tired. Ryan came❶ home very late last night."

"He was at the beach again," says Janet. "I saw his bike when I took Charlie for his late night walk."

Abi frowns. "He told me he was at his friend's house. It was five o'clock this morning when he came home."

"Well, dear, Ryan's a young man now. See you tomorrow."

Janet takes her change and leaves the shop.

There are many people walking up and down the street. Lynton is always a lively place on Saturdays. On her

Bei den meisten Verben bildet man die einfache Vergangenheitsform durch Anhängen der Endung **-ed**, aber viele häufige Verben sind unregelmäßig und man muss ihre Formen lernen:

come	→	came
be	→	was/were
do	→	did
leave	→	left
see	→	saw
take	→	took
tell	→	told

way home, Janet sees two more people she knows, Professor Timothy Stockholm and his personal trainer, Emily Cartwell. They are doing some stretching exercises. The professor is trying to get fit.

"Nice day for a run!" Janet says with a smile.

"It is never a nice day for running!" Timothy complains. "This woman is trying to kill me!"

stretching exercise	Dehnübung
to complain	(sich be)klagen
identification	Ausweispapiere
impatiently	ungeduldig
gossip	Klatsch
to hate	hassen

Emily frowns. "Less talking, more stretching!"

"Did Frank find out anything about the woman on the beach?" asks Janet. "Sophie says there was no identification on the body."

"No, nobody knows who she is – or was," Emily replies. "Frank waited there all morning to get an exclusive story. He's such a workaholic."

"At least it was nobody from the village," says the professor impatiently.

The two women are surprised by his words and his tone.

"It's tragic, of course," he continues, "but I don't think this gossip can answer any questions."

Timothy hates gossip. He is often in the news because his laboratory does experiments on animals. He knows that his work is important and helps people. But news reporters like to tell stories only in black and white. Some people even call him "Dr Frankenstein".

Exercise 4: Prepositions. Lesen Sie weiter und wählen Sie die richtige Präposition!

Back 1. at / on the police station in Barnstaple, Inspector Lloyd is explaining the situation 2. at / to a small team of officers. Everyone's eyes follow him as he walks up and 3. below / down the room.
"The time of death was 4. between / from midnight and two o'clock 5. in / on the morning. It looks like she didn't kill herself. There is **evidence** of a fight on top of the cliff, **including** many footprints. Someone with large shoes was there. There are also three **broken** fingernails 6. in / on her right hand. We found one 7. from / of them on the fence with the same red **nail varnish**."

The inspector puts photographs on the wall while he is speaking. There are rings of light skin on two of the woman's fingers.

"Do we know who she is?" asks **Detective Sergeant** Parker, a young woman from London.

In Großbritannien haben viele Geschäfte auch sonntags geöffnet und viele Familien erledigen dann den Wocheneinkauf.

Inspector Lloyd runs his hands through his hair.
"She wasn't a guest at any of the hotels or guesthouses. And we don't know of any **missing** people who look like her. Nobody found a handbag, money or a phone."

"So it was a mugging," Parker says. "The killer took everything, including her rings."

DS Parker doesn't have a very good imagination, thinks the inspector. She still has a lot to learn.

"Maybe," he says. "But a mugging in Lynton? And at that time of night?"

"All sorts of people visit the village," she explains impatiently. "And the pubs close between eleven and midnight. We think she died soon after that…?"

Inspector Lloyd looks at the photographs of the woman's

evidence	Hinweis, Beweismaterial
including	inklusive
broken	(ab)gebrochen
nail varnish	Nagellack
Detective Sergeant (DS)	Kriminalmeisterin
missing	vermisst
mugging	Überfall (auf offener Straβe)
imagination	Vorstellungskraft
security camera footage	Sicherheitskameraaufnahmen
case	*hier:* Fall
to be in a hurry	es eilig haben

broken nails again – and at the worse ones of her broken neck.

"That's true," he says slowly. "But let's find out who she is. Parker, take a team and talk to everyone in the village. Also find out who was in the pubs last night."

"Okay. I'll get all the security camera footage, too."

"Good. I need to work on another case for a while. There's a man in a caravan who is selling ecstasy up and down the coast."

The next morning, Abi Weston is in a hurry to get to work. Her three children are on holiday from school for seven weeks. Ryan, the oldest, should be babysitting his sisters, but he's not at home. Typical Ryan! While she is washing up, Abi sees smoke in the back garden.

"Oh, no!" she cries. "The neighbour's having a **bonfire** again. Our washing is still outside!"

Her daughter Hannah looks out of the window and sees her brother. "It's not the neighbours," she says. "It's Ryan."

Abi runs out of the kitchen and into the garden. On her way, she picks up the garden **hose**. She holds it in both hands like a pistol.

"What do you think you're doing, young man?" she shouts. Ryan looks shocked and then angry. "Leave me alone!"

"Are you blind? Do you want our clean clothes to smell of smoke?"

"I'm **burning** the **hedge cuttings**. You told me to do it!" he complains. "Why aren't you at work?"

Without speaking, Abi **points** the hose at her son and pulls the **trigger**. Cold water shoots him in the face. He **squeals** and jumps to one side. She sprays him again.

"Mum! Stop it! Are you crazy?"

"Don't be so **cheeky**!" she says. "Respect your mother."

bonfire	(Lager-)Feuer
hose	Schlauch
to burn	(ver)brennen
hedge cuttings *pl*	Heckenabschnitt
to point (at)	zeigen (auf), zielen (auf)
trigger	Auslöser, Abzug
to squeal	kreischen, quieken
cheeky	frech

Wenn sie mit ihrer Mutter reden, sagen die meisten Briten "Mum" oder "Ma", in den USA ist "Mom" üblich. Kleine Kinder sagen "Mummy". "Mother" ist beim Sprechen dagegen sehr formell.

"God!" he shouts. "You're so unfair!" His hair, jeans and T-shirt are all extremely wet.

Ryan runs past her into the house. Hannah is laughing at him when he enters the kitchen.

carefully	vorsichtig
chain	Kette

"You needed a good shower!"

Back in the garden, Abi is using the hose to put water on the fire. Some of the hedge cuttings are now black. Below them there is something that looks like metal. She **carefully** pulls a long, thin **chain** from the ashes. On the other end there is a burnt object with a metal logo on the front. It's an expensive ladies' handbag!

Exercise 5: Odd one out. Welches Wort ist das „schwarze Schaf"? Unterstreichen Sie das Wort, das nicht in die Reihe passt!

1. bonfire   smoke   washing   ashes
2. handbag   rings   chain   hose
3. to complain   to shout   to cry   to squeal
4. case   gossip   mugging   evidence

On the other side of the village, Frank Thomson is writing some articles for a local newspaper on his laptop. His girlfriend Emily is still in bed. He finishes a story about the suicide on Friday night, then he takes Emily a cup of coffee.

"It's Sunday," she says. "You shouldn't be working."

"I have to finish by midday tomorrow," he explains. "I didn't sleep all night."

"Really? I didn't notice. I slept like a baby again."

"Yeah, you always do after a long run," Frank laughs.

"Are you working on the story about Professor Stockholm?" she asks. "Did you hear from your contact?"

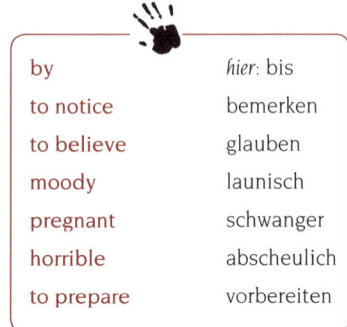

by	*hier*: bis
to notice	bemerken
to believe	glauben
moody	launisch
pregnant	schwanger
horrible	abscheulich
to prepare	vorbereiten

Frank frowns into his coffee. "No… but I hope to meet her later. She has all the extra information I need about his laboratory."

"I won't believe it until I see it with my own eyes," says Emily. "The professor's a nice man. Moody, but nice."

"Well, maybe he is," Frank replies. "But my contact says she has videos of his experiments on pregnant rabbits and mice. They put chemicals in the animals' food to see what happens to the babies – before and after they are born."

"That's horrible!"

"Yes, it is. But I'm sure the money's good," says Frank simply.

"What time are you meeting this mystery woman?"

"At four o'clock, and I have to meet her in Bristol. That's a two-hour drive." Frank looks at his watch. "I should leave soon."

"No, you should lie down and rest for a while," Emily says.

Frank smiles nervously and looks at his watch again.

"I have to finish preparing. I'll be okay."

Exercise 6: Crossword puzzle. Lösen Sie das Kreuzworträtsel!

Across

2. Very bad; not kind or ethical.
5. A long plastic object you use to water a garden.
6. Abi ... the hose at Ryan.
7. A problem or mystery that the police work on.

Down

1. Something you often eat for breakfast.
2. A married man.
3. Not later than: "I have to finish ... 5 p.m. today."
4. Facts or objects that make you think something is true.

Secrets in Bristol

Early on Monday morning, Inspector Lloyd is standing in an elegant **flat** in Bristol with DS Parker. There are modern pictures on the walls, but no personal photographs. Every room is clean and well organized. On the kitchen table, next to the toaster, there are lots of newspaper articles, **maps** and pictures.

flat	Wohnung
map	Landkarte
screenshot	Bildschirmfoto
disgusting	ekelhaft

"What do you think these are?" asks DS Parker.

"Hmm. The quality of the pictures is very bad. They look like **screenshots** from a video. Green countryside. Some buildings. Lots of animals… a farm? No, wait, there are cats in this one. Dogs. Lots of mice and rats. Rabbits…," the inspector pauses and frowns at the picture in his hand.

"Experiments?" asks the sergeant.

"It's a laboratory," he says without emotion. "**Disgusting**."

"So it's definitely the woman you're looking for, is it?" asks a tall officer in uniform. He has a strong regional accent

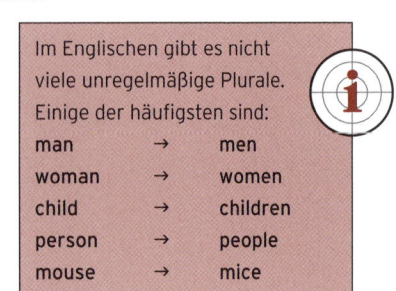

Im Englischen gibt es nicht viele unregelmäßige Plurale. Einige der häufigsten sind:

man	→	men
woman	→	women
child	→	children
person	→	people
mouse	→	mice

and is standing patiently by the front door.

dental records *pl*	Zahnarztunterlagen
to confirm	bestätigen
to rent	mieten
animal rights activist	Tierschützerin

"Yes," replies Inspector Lloyd, "we found her passport in the bedroom. Christina Montague, age twenty-seven. The **dental records** will **confirm** her identity."

"We'll wait to contact her parents," says the officer. "They live in Northern Ireland, and so did she. She started **renting** this place last month, but her life was in Belfast."

"What else do you know about her?" asks DS Parker.

"Well, we talked to the neighbour who reported her missing. Ms[i] Montague was an **animal rights activist**. She was here to collect evidence about some laboratories in the South West of England."

The doorbell rings. The officer turns and opens the door.

"There's something I forgot to tell you, Officer," the neighbour says. "A man came here last night to talk to Christina. A journalist. He rang my bell when Christina didn't answer hers."

"Did Ms Montague have many visitors?" asks Inspector Lloyd.

"No, not at all. I never heard anyone else in the flat."

"I have some more questions, madam," says the inspector. "Parker, now that we have a name and an address, you can check Ms Montague's

> Mit **Ms** (Frau) kann man sowohl unverheiratete wie verheiratete Frauen anreden. Besonders wenn man nicht weiβ, ob die angesprochene Dame verheiratet ist, ist diese Anrede neutral. **Miss** benutzt man für junge Mädchen und unverheiratete Frauen.

phone records. We need to give her laptop to our computer specialists, too."

> **Exercise 7: Spelling mistakes.** Lesen Sie weiter, unterstreichen Sie die sechs Schreibfehler im Text und verbessern Sie sie!
>
> Back in Lynton, Timothy Stockholm is jogging with Emily Cartwell. After runing for ten minutes, he is all ready very tired and **out of breath**.
> They arrive at the bottom of the **path** through the woods.
> "I don't want to go up there," says the proffessor.
> He is now walking slowly with one hand on his fat belly.
> "You can do it!" Emily says enthusiastically. "Come on!"
> She takes twenty stepps up the hill and looks back. Timothy is not moving. He is **staring at** the top of the cliff.
> "No!" he shouts angryly. "I'm going home!"
> Emily lets him go; it is almost the end of there workout.
>
> 1. _____ 2. _____
> 3. _____ 4. _____
> 5. _____ 6. _____

On the way back to his house, Timothy walks through the village. Outside the shop, he stops in shock when he sees a familiar face and reads the words: "Body identified!"

Frank Thomson is stressed. It's after two o'clock in the afternoon and his article for the local newspaper isn't ready. He still doesn't have any evidence that Professor Stockholm's laboratory is doing illegal experiments. Why did Christina have to ruin everything? She was such a manipulative woman! The phone rings.

phone records *pl*	Telefonverbindungsdaten
out of breath	außer Atem
path	Pfad
to stare at	starren auf
instead	stattdessen
murder	Mord
to have no idea	keine Ahnung haben

"Where's your story, Frank?" his boss asks.

"I need another day. Like I said in my email, we can't print the article without any pictures or specific details."

"Oh, yes, I remember. That's fine," his boss replies. He does not sound angry. "We'll put it on the front page next week. I want you to concentrate on that woman in Lynton **instead**."

"The suicide of an unknown person?" Frank asks.

"Good god, man! Don't you listen to the news? The police identified her this morning. They think it was **murder**."

"I… I **had no idea**! I'll find out everything I can."

"Yes, do that. Call me back around six with an update."

Abi Weston finishes washing up after lunch. Then she gives her three children some money to go to the swimming pool.

> Sammelbegriffe wie **the police** beschreiben eine Gruppe von mehreren Personen. Deshalb verwendet man wie hier die Personalpronomen in der 3. Person Plural, um sie zu ersetzen. Andere Beispiele sind *team, family* und *audience*.

"Do I have to go?" complains Ryan.

"Yes, you do. Don't come back before dinner!"

Exercise 8: Definitions. Welches Wort aus dem vorangehenden Textabschnitt wird beschrieben?

1. a small group of shops and houses _____
2. a report of new information _____
3. the killing of a person _____
4. to look at for a long time _____

Once the house is empty, Abi puts a plastic bag on the kitchen table. She **feels sick**. Was it really the same person? Inside the burnt handbag, there is a leather **purse**. It is also **damaged** by the fire. There are some bank cards with an exotic name inside and a **driving licence**. The photo on the licence shows a young woman. It is definitely the same person.

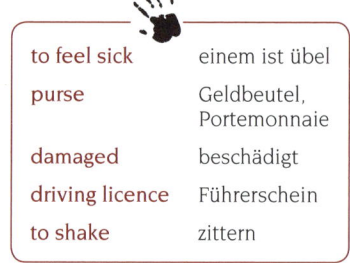

to feel sick	einem ist übel
purse	Geldbeutel, Portemonnaie
damaged	beschädigt
driving licence	Führerschein
to shake	zittern

"Oh, Ryan," she says to herself. "What have you done?"

Abi nervously lights a cigarette and opens a news website on the family computer. She starts to read articles about the woman.

Minutes later, she picks up the phone. Her hands are **shaking**, and so are her words when she begins to speak: "I have to talk to you about my son."

4. A Killer in Lynton

Early on Monday evening, Inspector Lloyd and DS Parker arrive at Emily Cartwell and Frank Thomson's house. Frank invites them into the kitchen to talk.

"Oh! You go ahead," says the inspector, "I just need to **tie my laces**."

He stays in the hall for a moment. Frank and Emily have lots of shoes and trainers there. DS Parker can start interviewing the journalist, he thinks. He does not like asking questions to people he knows from work.

"Where were you on Friday night, Mr Thomson?"

"Me?" Frank looks **confused**. "I was here with Emily. She went jogging between nine and ten. Then we watched a film before going to bed. Why do you ask?"

to tie one's laces	sich die Schnürsenkel binden
confused	verwirrt

"We know that you spoke to Christina Montague on the phone on Friday. You called each other more than ten times this month. Can you explain that?"

"Yes, of course… I still can't believe it was her," says Frank. He sounds sad. "She had some information for me about a laboratory near here. We studied together in Belfast. She was a journalist, too. Did you know that?"

The sergeant ignores his question. "When did you last meet Miss Montague?"

"Ages ago! It was in Northern Ireland after our university days."

Inspector Lloyd quietly walks into the kitchen. "How did Miss Montague get her information?"

⚡ ages ago	vor einer Ewigkeit
certainly	sicher(lich)
relationship	Beziehung
to repeat	wiederholen

"She worked undercover at one of Stockholm's laboratories earlier this year," explains Frank. "I'm not sure where."

DS Parker writes something down.

"Miss Montague's neighbour told us that you went to Bristol late on Sunday afternoon," she says. "Why didn't you see her in Lynton when she came on Friday?"

"I had no idea she was here!" Frank replies. "We wanted to meet on Sunday evening. I drove all the way to Bristol, but she wasn't there. You can ask her neighbour – I spoke to her. I'm sorry, but you should ask the professor about Friday."

"We will certainly talk to Professor Stockholm," the inspector says. "But first I have to ask you about your relationship with Christina Montague. It won't take long."

Exercise 9: Fill in the blanks. Lesen Sie weiter und ergänzen Sie den Text mit den fehlenden Wörtern!

| taxi | facts | car | alcohol | buses | July |

On the short drive to Timothy Stockholm's house, DS Parker repeats some of the most important **1.** _____ .

"Christina Montague hired a 2. _____ when she came to England in 3. _____. I'm sure that car is close to the village somewhere. There are no good trains to Bristol and the 4. _____ are very slow on these roads along the coast."

"Maybe she used a 5. _____ on Friday," the inspector replies. "She was rich, and there was 6. _____ in her blood."

"Hmm. But why was she here? It can't be a coincidence that Frank Thomson and Timothy Stockholm live in the same village, can it? Did she come to see one of them? Or both of them? When we interviewed people at the weekend, the professor said he was at home alone on Friday night."

Inspector Lloyd stops the car and gets out.

"You can ask him all of your questions yourself, Parker. He'll talk more to a nice young lady," he says with a smile.

As they are walking up to Professor Stockholm's front door, there is a loud bark. A dog runs up behind the inspector.

"Good evening!" says Janet Drummond. "Inspector, I need to talk to you."

"Can it wait?" asks DS Parker.

| to hire | mieten |
| coincidence | Zufall |

"No. I need to tell you what I know about Ryan Weston."

"What do you know?" the inspector asks.

"He was definitely at the beach late on Friday night. I saw his bike, and I heard him shouting with a girl or woman. Now his mother is phoning his friends' parents and asking all sorts of questions. The boy doesn't have an alibi!"

DS Parker frowns at the inspector. "Shall I go and visit the Weston family?"

"No, I'll go. You talk to Stockholm. Find out *everything*. Now, Mrs Drummond, please tell me exactly what you saw."

folded across one's chest	vor der Brust verschränkt
foolish	töricht
gesture	Geste
serious	ernst
size	Größe
to mutter	murmeln

Abi Weston is crying at the kitchen table. Ryan is sitting next to her with his arms **folded across his chest**.

"I found it!" he says loudly. "I found the handbag on the beach on my way home. It looked expensive. It was full of money. I didn't know what to do."

"Give it to the police?" Inspector Lloyd asks simply. "So you took the money and burnt everything else. **Foolish** boy!"

"He doesn't know right from wrong, Inspector," Abi says.

"Why were you there so late?" the inspector continues.

"I can't tell you that," Ryan answers.

"Listen. Mrs Drummond told me about a caravan. I believe the person in that caravan is selling ecstasy. Your bike was on the ground next to it."

Abi stares at Ryan. There is fire in her eyes.

"What!? Is this true?" she shouts.

Inspector Lloyd makes a slow **gesture** with his hand.

"This is very **serious**," he begins, "but not as serious as the murder of a young woman. That's right, isn't it, Mr Weston?"

Ryan looks down at his arms and doesn't answer. "Mr Weston, can you tell me what **size** shoes you wear?"

"An eight,"[i] he **mutters**. "Why?"

"I don't believe you killed anyone," replies the inspector. "I'm going to leave you two alone to talk. We'll see each other again very soon at the station. Help the police find the man in the caravan, Mr Weston, then we can help you."

Britische Schuh- und Kleidergrößen unterscheiden sich von deutschen. Die britische Schuhgröße 8 entspricht Größe 42.

As the inspector walks back to his car, he hears shouting from the Westons' house.

Exercise 10: Opposites. Wie lautet das Gegenteil der folgenden Begriffe?

1. to sell   _____
2. cheap   _____
3. early   _____
4. the most   _____

Inspector Lloyd drives back to the professor's house. He calls the station while he waits for DS Parker. The computer specialists should know something by now, he thinks.

"Well?" the inspector asks DS Parker when she gets into the car. "What did our friend Professor Stockholm tell you?"

to disappear	verschwinden
honest	ehrlich
to tell the truth	die Wahrheit sagen
voice	Stimme

"He says that he knew Christina," DS Parker begins. "She worked in his laboratory for two days last month, then she disappeared. She wasn't the first person to leave in her first week. He thought her name was Josephine Gardener. He seems very shocked about her death."

"What about his laboratory? Is that where the screenshots in Christina's flat came from?"

"Yes, he confirmed that. He says that a lot of people hate the idea of his experiments, but his work isn't illegal. Actually, [i] he likes to be honest and transparent. People don't normally see all the details, of course…"

"So he has no clear motive," the inspector continues.

"No. And he says he went to bed before midnight," replies Parker. "What about Ryan Weston?"

"He's a foolish boy, that's all. I think he's buying and selling drugs for his friends. That's why he isn't telling

Vorsicht "Falsche Freunde"!
actually = eigentlich
current(ly) = aktuell

the truth to anyone. He found Christina's handbag and took her money. But he didn't know that she was dead. And Janet Drummond didn't see him; she only heard voices on top of the cliff."

"Voices? Who was there?" asks Parker.

"You'll see. We're going to talk to him again now."

DS Parker is confused. She frowns and thinks for a moment. "Of course! Frank Thomson knew Christina."
"Yes," says Inspector Lloyd. "They knew each other. They knew each other *very* well."

Emily Cartwell answers the door in her pyjamas. She is shocked to see the police so late.
"I'm sorry to disturb you, Miss Cartwell," Inspector Lloyd begins. "We need to speak to Mr Thomson again."
"I have nothing new to tell you," says Frank. He is standing behind his girlfriend in shorts and a T-shirt.

to disturb	stören
to hide	verbergen, verstecken
to raise	hochziehen
recent	neu, aus jüngster Zeit

"Can we talk alone?" asks the inspector.
"No," says Frank. "I have nothing to hide. I want Emily to hear everything."
"Very well," Inspector Lloyd continues. "Can you explain why there are hundreds of photos of you on Christina Montague's laptop?"
Frank raises his eyebrows in surprise and says nothing.
"Many of them are years old, but some are very recent. There are pictures of you both in Bristol last month, for example. She also had a collection of articles in her kitchen – stories that you wrote. They weren't all about animals."
"Was she in love with you, Mr Thomson?" asks DS Parker.
"I don't have to answer these questions," says Frank. "As you know, I was here with Emily when that woman died."

Emily's face is now red and there are tears in her eyes. She remembers falling asleep during the film… should she say something?

"You knew that Miss Montague was undercover," DS Parker continues. "Why did she tell you that? What did she want for the information?"

Frank **remains silent**.

"Not many people wear size twelve shoes, Mr Thomson. I know that you do because I looked when we visited earlier. The footprints we found on top of the cliff were the same size. Were you there late on Friday night?"

Emily stares at Frank. He's biting his lip, she notices. He always does that when he's thinking about what to write or what to say.

"Frank! Say something!" she shouts.

"We can always take your shoes to our specialists and ask them to find out," says DS Parker.

"It was an **accident**," replies Frank slowly. "She fell."

"No! What?" Emily **gasps**.

"She fell. Christina was crazy. She hated to see me happy with someone new."

"Someone *new*?" asks Emily. "When were you with her?"

"Ages ago, in Belfast…," mutters Frank. His voice is shaking.

Emily feels sick.

to remain silent	schweigen
accident	Unfall
to gasp	keuchen

"Yes," says Inspector Lloyd. "We have emails and pictures to confirm that. But why did she come here all the way from Northern Ireland?"

"She wanted to help me get information about Stockholm."
"What else did she want?" asks DS Parker. "Why did she come to Lynton so late on Friday night?"
Frank is sweating now. "She called on Friday evening and asked to see me," he explains. "I thought it was about the laboratory, but she gave me an ultimatum. I could have the information for my article, but first I had to spend the weekend with her."
"Why is this article so important?" asks Inspector Lloyd.
"Well, it isn't. We argued

to sweat	schwitzen
to spend	*hier*: verbringen
to argue	sich streiten
manslaughter	fahrlässige Tötung
drunk	betrunken
to hit sb.	jmd. schlagen

for a long time. I tried to tell her that we had no future together. I told her that Emily is more important to me than an exclusive story. I walked away, but Christina followed me all the way up to the top of the cliff."
"And so you pushed her into the fence and watched her fall?" asks the inspector. "That's manslaughter."
"She was drunk!" Frank cries. "She hit me first!"
Emily is crying loudly. "You monster! You killed her and went back first thing in the morning!"
She turns and runs upstairs.
Frank can only watch her go.
"Why didn't you call for an ambulance? And why did you make it look like a mugging?" Inspector Lloyd asks.
"I… I panicked," says Frank. He also has tears in his eyes.

"Stop crying," DS Parker says impatiently. "It's too late for that. A woman is dead and you are responsible."

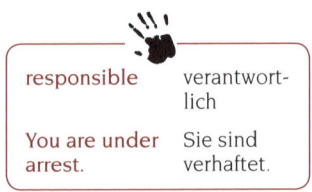

| responsible | verantwortlich |
| You are under arrest. | Sie sind verhaftet. |

Inspector Lloyd stares at the journalist. "You are under arrest, Mr Thomson. You do not have to say anything…"

"I know!" says Frank angrily. "Emily! I love you!" he shouts. But there is no sound from upstairs.

Exercise 11: Translation quiz. Übersetzen Sie die Wörter ins Englische und enträtseln Sie das Lösungswort!

1. verschwinden   _ _ _ ☐ _ _ _ _ _
2. ehrlich   _ _ ☐ _ _ _
3. Unfall   _ _ _ ☐ _ _ _ _
4. schweigen   _ _ ☐ _ _ _ _ _ _ _ _ _
5. schwitzen   _ _ _ ☐ _
6. Nagellack   _ _ _ ☐ _ _ _ _ _ ☐ _

Hidden word: _ _ _ _ _ _ _

Death at the Lake

Caroline Simpson

1. A Noise in the Night

It's an early Saturday evening in July. Simon and his girlfriend Wendy are sitting outside their **tent**. They are watching the sun go down over Derwentwater.

"It's so beautiful and quiet here, isn't it?" says Simon.

"Yes, but are you sure it's okay for us to camp here by the lake all alone?"

"Don't worry, Wendy. We're not doing anything wrong. Just look at that **view**."

noise	Geräusch
tent	Zelt
view	Ausblick, Aussicht
to point (to)	zeigen auf
island	Insel
to whisper	flüstern
voice	Stimme

He **points to** the green Catsbells hills behind them. "That's the perfect place for hiking. The view from the top is fantastic. And look, that's Hawes End Pier in front of us. And over there in the middle of the lake is St. Herbert's **island**."

"Yes, you're right. It is beautiful here," she answers.

"Wake up, Simon! There's something out there," Wendy **whispers** a few hours later.

Derwentwater ist der viertgrößte See Englands und liegt im **Lake District**, einem Nationalpark und beliebten Urlaubsgebiet im Nordwesten Englands.

"What…?" he answers in a sleepy **voice**.

"A noise! Outside the tent!"

She opens the front of the tent and looks out into the darkness.

"It's probably just an animal. Go back to sleep, Wendy."

"No, I can't sleep now. Please, Simon. Just go and look."

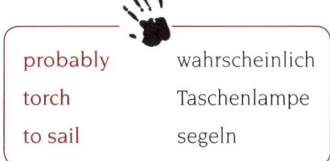

probably	wahrscheinlich
torch	Taschenlampe
to sail	segeln

"Okay, but after that you must let me sleep." He puts on some shoes and a jacket, picks up his torch and goes outside.

Nervously, Wendy sits alone in the dark tent and waits. After a while she looks at her watch in the light from her torch.

I hope Simon comes back soon, she thinks. Again she hears something. Oh god, it's coming nearer!

The front of the tent opens and Wendy screams.

"Calm down. It's only me," Simons says. "I looked all around the tent. There's nothing there. Now please, can we get some sleep?"

Exercise 1: Missing words. Lesen Sie weiter und ergänzen Sie die fehlenden Wörter!

side   lake   sun   water   boat

"Next stop Hawes End Pier," says the captain as the small tourist **1.** sails slowly around the **2.** . It's 10:20 a.m. on Sunday morning. The **3.** is shining and Little Tommy is playing with a stick over the **4.** of the boat. He fishes something out of the **5.** .

"Be careful, Tommy," his father says. "Don't fall in."
"Daddy, look what I found in the lake," Tommy replies and shows him a red scarf. "And over there by the pier... there's something else."
The boat stops at the lake side. Tommy's father gets out to take a closer look. When he comes back, his face is white.

careful	vorsichtig
to reply	antworten
scarf	Schal
body	*hier*: Leiche
Detective Inspector (DI)	Kriminalkommissarin
local	einheimisch
Detective Sergeant (DS)	Kriminalmeister
strange	seltsam
to rob sb.	jmd. ausrauben
meanwhile	in der Zwischenzeit

"Quick, someone help! There's a body in the water!"

Half an hour later, two police officers are standing by the lake. A forensic team is photographing the body.
"You live near here, don't you, Atkinson?" says Detective Inspector Linda McKenzie. "Do you know who she was?"
"Yes," the younger officer tells his boss. "She's Rosie Chapman, a local girl, 19 years old. Her family lives over there in Keswick." Detective Sergeant Atkinson points to the other side of the lake. "Rosie is a student at Carlisle University... I mean, she was... Poor Rosie!"
"It's strange that she had nothing with her... no bag or phone. Perhaps somebody robbed her. Or perhaps her things are still in the water. We need to search the lake," McKenzie says. "Atkinson, I think you should tell the family about Rosie. You know them well. Meanwhile, I can take a look around here."

At midday, DS Atkinson rings the doorbell at Dr and Mrs Chapman's house in Keswick. Mrs Chapman opens the door and smiles at him. "Come in, Sergeant," she says. "How can we help you?"

terrible	furchtbar
confused	verwirrt
What's going on?	Was ist los?
husband	Ehemann
wife	Ehefrau
to wipe	wischen, abtrocknen

"I… I'm sorry… it's about Rosie," he says slowly.

"Rosie? Oh, she's probably still asleep," Mrs Chapman says with a laugh. "She was out late last night with her friends."

"I have some terrible news," says Atkinson sadly. "We found her this morning at Hawes End Pier… I'm sorry, she's dead!"

Mrs Chapman looks confused. "No, that must be a mistake. Wait here a moment."

She runs upstairs and knocks on Rosie's bedroom door. No answer. She opens the door. The room is empty.

She comes back downstairs to the living room in shock.

"What's going on?" her husband asks.

Atkinson takes Mrs Chapman's arm and helps her walk to the sofa. "Please sit down. I need to ask you both some questions. Where was Rosie last night?"

Mrs Chapman is crying and cannot speak. Dr Chapman puts his arm around his wife.

"Rosie came home from university for the weekend," he says. "Her friend Annabelle invited her to a party."

"Where was the party?" Atkinson asks.

"At the Loft Nightclub, you know, behind the King's Arms Hotel," he says and wipes his eyes. "She left here at 9 p.m."

"How was Rosie when she left?"

"Happy. **Looking forward to** seeing her friends again."
"How did she get to the nightclub?" Atkinson asks him.
"On her bike."
"What did she take with her? A bag maybe?"

to look forward to	sich auf etwas freuen
shaky	zittrig
ID card	Ausweis

Dr Chapman shakes his head. "I don't know that."
"She always carries her phone and money in her pink rucksack," says Mrs Chapman in a **shaky** voice. She covers her face with her hands.
"I'm sorry, but I need to look at Rosie's room," says Atkinson.
"Yes, of course," says Dr Chapman and takes him upstairs.

Exercise 2: Relationship matching. Ergänzen Sie die fehlenden Begriffe zu den Beziehungen der Charaktere!

wife   boss   daughter   boyfriend

1. Rosie is Mrs Chapman's _____.
2. Simon is Wendy's _____.
3. DI McKenzie is DS Atkinson's _____.
4. Mrs Chapman is Dr Chapman's _____.

"Good afternoon," McKenzie says to two campers who are sitting outside their tent, drinking tea. "Can I ask you a few questions?" She shows them her **ID card**.
Simon looks worried. "Have we done something wrong?"

"No, sir," McKenzie answers. "We are **investigating** a **crime**. We found a body in the lake this morning. Did you see or hear anything strange last night?"

to investigate	ermitteln
crime	Verbrechen
about	*hier*: circa
past	*hier*: vorbei (an)
scared	verängstigt
to agree	zustimmen
to nod	nicken
diary	Tagebuch

"Yes!" says Wendy. "At **about** 2:30 a.m. I heard a noise outside the tent, like someone walking **past**. I asked Simon to go and look."

"Did you see anyone?" McKenzie asks Simon.

"No, I looked all around but no one was there," he answers.

"What about this morning? Did you see anything strange?"

"No, nothing. We had breakfast and relaxed here by the tent," Wendy answers. "Simon, please let's go somewhere else for the rest of our holiday. I'm too **scared** to stay here."

"Okay," he **agrees**. "We could go to a hotel."

"I need your names and telephone numbers, please," says McKenzie. "And let me know where you are staying."

At 2 o'clock, McKenzie meets Atkinson outside the King's Arms Hotel in Keswick.

"Did you find anything in Rosie Chapman's room?" she asks.

Atkinson **nods** and hands her a book.

"It's her **diary**," he says. "I found it under her bed."

"Very interesting," McKenzie replies as they go inside.

"Hello. What would you like to drink?" asks a young man who is standing behind the bar.

"Hello, Martin," says Atkinson. "This is DI McKenzie. We want to ask you some questions. You work at the Loft Nightclub in the evenings, don't you?"

"Yes, that's right," Martin Brady replies.

"We want to know about the party last night. Was Rosie Chapman there?" asks McKenzie.

"Yes, she was. She and her friends had a great time. They were laughing, drinking and dancing. But then she and Dean **had an argument**."

to have an argument	sich streiten
hothead	Hitzkopf
closing time	Sperrstunde
to remember	sich erinnern

"Who's Dean?" McKenzie asks.

"Rosie's boyfriend," the barman answers. "He's a real **hothead**. He often has fights here at **closing time**."

"What was the argument about?" McKenzie asks.

"I don't know. I couldn't hear. The music was too loud."

"What happened next?"

Exercise 3: Unscramble the text. Lesen Sie weiter und bringen Sie die Sätze in die richtige Reihenfolge!

a) "About 1 o'clock in the morning."
b) "Please give us a list of people who were at the club last night. Everyone you can **remember**," says McKenzie.
c) "What time was that?" Atkinson asks.
d) "Rosie left alone. A few minutes later Dean left, too."

1	2	3	4

The Missing Suspect

Outside the hotel, McKenzie phones the police station.

"Hello Cartwright. McKenzie here. Please contact these people and ask them to come in for questioning."

She gives the WPC the names on Martin Brady's list. "Now, let's visit Dean Watson," she tells Atkinson. "You know his address, don't you?"

"Yes, I do. He's often in trouble. He lives about two miles from here."

While Atkinson is driving, McKenzie opens Rosie's diary and starts to read.

"Listen to this, Atkinson. 'It's all over between me and Dean. But I'm scared to tell

missing	*hier*: verschwunden, vermisst
suspect	Verdächtiger
to come in for questioning	zur Vernehmung erscheinen
WPC (Woman Police Constable)	Polizistin
trouble	Schwierigkeiten
elderly	ältere

him. What can I do?' That's the last thing Rosie wrote in her diary on Friday. The day before the party. How interesting."

They arrive at 15 Ambleside Road, park the car and walk up to the front door.

"Strange that the curtains on the ground floor are closed," McKenzie says. "It looks like no one is home."

"You're right. He's not home," says an elderly woman who is standing by the flower beds in the front garden.

"Good afternoon. We are DI McKenzie and DS Atkinson of the Penrith police. We want to talk to Dean Watson."

"**Oh dear!** Is he in trouble again? I'm Mrs Price, Dean's landlady. I live upstairs," the woman explains.

Oh dear!	Oh je!
as... as...	so ... wie ...
dustbin	Mülltonne
purse	Geldbeutel
search warrant	Durchsuchungsbefehl
to put out an APB (all points bulletin)	zur Fahndung ausschreiben

"When did you last see Dean, Mrs Price?" McKenzie asks.

"Yesterday evening at around 9 p.m. He said he was going to the nightclub. I didn't hear or see him come home."

"Thank you. Here's my card. Please call us **as** soon **as** Mr Watson comes back," says McKenzie.

Mrs Price walks with them towards the street. She opens the **dustbin** in the garden to throw something away.

"Wait a minute," says McKenzie. "What's that?"

"Someone left this in my garden," says Mrs Price.

She shows the officers a dirty, pink rucksack.

"Where exactly did you find this?" McKenzie asks.

"Over there, in my rose bushes."

McKenzie takes a look inside the bag. There is a **purse**. She opens it carefully. Inside is a bank card with the name Rosie Chapman on it.

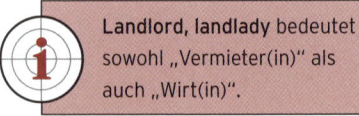

Landlord, landlady bedeutet sowohl „Vermieter(in)" als auch „Wirt(in)".

McKenzie takes out her phone. "Cartwright. Get a **search warrant** for 15 Ambleside Road. And **put out an APB** for Dean Watson. What? Okay, we are coming back now."

She turns to Atkinson. "Some of Rosie's friends are already waiting for questioning. Let's get back to the station right away. Mrs Price, we'll take the rucksack with us. Thank you for your help."

already	schon, bereits
right away	sofort
opposite	gegenüber
I'm afraid so.	Ich fürchte ja.
lovely	herrlich
to believe	glauben
scholarship	Stipendium

Exercise 4: Translating adjectives. Ordnen Sie den Adjektiven die passende Übersetzung zu!

1. ☐ strange   a) verängstigt
2. ☐ dirty   b) älterer
3. ☐ scared   c) seltsam
4. ☐ elderly   d) dreckig

At 4 p.m. McKenzie and Atkinson sit down opposite Annabelle Newton in an interview room at Penrith police station. Annabelle is crying and her eyes are red.
"Is it true that Rosie is dead?" she asks them.
"I'm afraid so," answers McKenzie.
"It's terrible. Only yesterday we were all together. It was a lovely evening. I can't believe that she is dead."
"It was your party at the Loft, wasn't it, Ms Newton?"
"Yes, I've got a scholarship to study Medicine at King's College, London. I wanted to celebrate with my best friends," she replies in a shaky voice.
"Tell us about the party. Did Rosie seem alright?"

"She was fine at first. We had a good time."

"What do you mean, 'at first'? Did something happen later?"

"This is not easy for me, Inspector," Annabelle answers. "Dean is an old friend, too. I don't like to say anything bad about him…"

"Please tell us everything you know," McKenzie says.

"Well, around midnight Dean started an argument with Rosie. He said she thinks she is better than him now because she is at university."

"What did Rosie say?" Atkinson asks.

"At first she just ignored him. She was reading messages on her phone. That made Dean even angrier. He started shouting at her 'You have another boyfriend!' That's when Rosie got up and left. She said she was going home."

"So she left alone?" asks McKenzie.

Annabelle nods.

"What about Dean?"

"We told him to calm down. But he was really angry. After a couple of minutes, he left, too."

> Das Wort **couple** bedeutet sowohl *Paar* als auch *paar*. Mit *paar* wird die Präposition **of** verwendet, z.B. *I've got a couple of questions.*

"Ms Newton, do you have any idea where Dean could be now?" McKenzie asks.

Annabelle shakes her head sadly.

"Thank you. That's all for now," says McKenzie.

At 7 p.m. the two officers are walking to the forensic lab.

"All the party guests say the same thing," McKenzie says. "Dean was angry at Rosie. She left alone and he followed her. And now he's missing, too. That's very suspicious."

"Plus Rosie's rucksack was in his garden in the rose bushes," says Atkinson.
"We must find him as soon as possible."
They arrive at a large grey building and go inside.

> **Exercise 5: True or false?** Welche Aussagen sind korrekt? Markieren Sie mit richtig ✔ oder falsch – !
>
> 1. Atkinson doesn't know where Dean lives. ☐
> 2. Dean is not at home. ☐
> 3. Mrs Price finds Rosie's bicycle in her garden. ☐
> 4. Rosie and Dean left the nightclub together. ☐

"Good evening, Officers," says a tall man in a doctor's coat. "Please follow me."
They go into a lab. In the middle of it, Rosie's body is lying on a table.
"What can you tell us so far, Dr Abbott?" asks McKenzie. Abbott pulls back a sheet to show the dead woman.
"Rosie Chapman died at about 2 a.m. on Sunday morning," says the doctor. "She has a cut on her head

lab (laboratory)	Labor
suspicious	verdächtig
building	Gebäude
sheet	Laken
cut	Schnittwunde
broken	gebrochen
mark	Fleck, Schramme
to hit sb.	*hier*: mit jmd. zusammenstoßen
scratch	Kratzer

and a broken leg. Look at these marks. It looks like a car hit her. And do you see these scratches on her arms and legs?

I think someone pulled her over the ground and threw her into the lake. There was no water in her lungs. So she was dead already."

McKenzie takes out a map of Derwentwater.

"But why was Rosie at Hawes End? She told her friends that she wanted to go home. Her parents' house is near the nightclub in the town centre. Hawes End lies the other way, four miles to the west. Why was she there?"

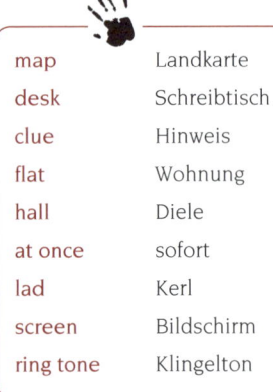

map	Landkarte
desk	Schreibtisch
clue	Hinweis
flat	Wohnung
hall	Diele
at once	sofort
lad	Kerl
screen	Bildschirm
ring tone	Klingelton

It's early Monday morning at 15 Ambleside Road, and McKenzie is in Dean Watson's living room. She is searching his desk. Atkinson walks in from the bedroom.

"Did you find anything?" he asks.

"No," McKenzie answers, frustrated. "There are no clues here. Nothing to tell us where he is. Let's get back to the station."

The officers leave the flat and see Mrs Price in the hall.

"Is there any news about Dean?" she asks.

"Not at the moment, Mrs Price," McKenzie answers. "If you see him, please let us know at once."

On, in und at zählen zu den häufigsten Präpositionen im Englischen. Sie können sowohl Orts- als auch Zeitangaben machen:

z.B. *on the table / on Monday*
in the living room / in August
at home / at the weekend

"Of course, Inspector," the elderly woman replies. "Dean's often in trouble. But he's a good lad, you know."

Exercise 6: Prepositions. Lesen Sie weiter und ergänzen Sie die fehlenden Präpositionen!

in   on   at   in   on

Meanwhile **1.** _____ the King's Arms Hotel, Simon is taking a shower. Wendy is **2.** _____ bed. She is watching the local news **3.** _____ TV.

"Yesterday morning a tourist found the body of a young woman **4.** _____ Derwentwater," the news reporter says. "Rosie Chapman was only 19 years old."

Wendy sees a photo of a young woman with long dark hair and a big smile **5.** _____ the TV screen.

"If anyone has any information, please contact the Penrith police station at this telephone number..."

Just then, Wendy hears music. It is coming from Simon's rucksack.

That's strange, she thinks. Did Simon change his ring tone?

> Achtung, falscher Freund! Im Englischen wird das Wort **handy** nur als Adjektiv verwendet *(praktisch, griffbereit)* und nicht als Bezeichnung für ein Mobiltelefon *(mobile phone)*.

"Simon, your phone is ringing!" she shouts.

"I'm still in the shower. Can you answer it?"

Wendy opens his bag and sees a pink mobile phone.

What's this? she thinks. It isn't Simon's phone! The screensaver is a selfie of a young couple who are laughing happily. The man has short blonde hair and round glasses, and the woman…

That's the woman in the news! Wendy thinks in shock.

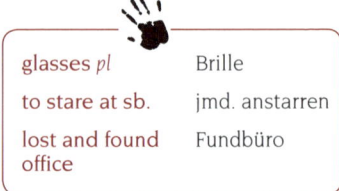

glasses *pl*	Brille
to stare at sb.	jmd. anstarren
lost and found office	Fundbüro

Simon comes out of the bathroom. Wendy is still holding the phone and stares at him.

"Where did you get this?" she asks.

"I found it when we packed the tent. I'm going to take it to the lost and found office after breakfast."

"Simon, a young woman is dead. And this is her phone. We must go to the police station at once!"

3. The Mysterious J

"Inspector McKenzie, I'm glad you're back!" WPC Cartwright says in an excited voice.

"What's the matter, Cartwright?"

"It's Dean Watson... He's here... in the waiting room."

excited	aufgeregt
to hurry	sich beeilen
voice recorder	Diktiergerät

"Really? Now that's quite a surprise!"

McKenzie and Atkinson hurry into the next room. They see a young man with dark hair and a cut on his face. He looks very tired and sad.

"Is it true about Rosie?" he asks. "I heard it on the radio."

"Dean Watson?" McKenzie asks. "Please follow me."

The officers take him into an interview room and close the door. McKenzie turns on a voice recorder.

"Now, Mr Watson, what happened on Saturday night?"

"Do you think I killed her?" Dean asks in horror.

"We know that you and Rosie had an argument at the nightclub on Saturday. Now tell us about it."

"Alright. I shouted at her and she left. I was angry but I was sorry, too. I wanted to talk to her. So I followed her."

"What time was this?" Atkinson asks.

"About 1 a.m., I think. It was like this: I leave the Loft and drive down the road towards Rosie's house. Then I see her on her bike. But she doesn't turn left to her house. She goes right towards Eleven Trees Lane. And I follow her."

ancient	sehr alt
to add	ergänzen
lovers' lane	lauschiges, romantisches Plätzchen
to overtake	überholen
to hit sb.	*hier*: jmd. schlagen

"Eleven Trees Lane?" asks McKenzie.

"That's a small country road," Atkinson explains. "It goes out of the town and up to the hills. On the top is an ancient stone circle."

"Yes, the Castlerigg Stone Circle," Dean adds. "Rosie and I went there often. It's like a lovers' lane for the young people here... a little scary, but romantic."

"Please go on with your story," McKenzie says.

"Okay, I overtake her and get out of the car. I say, Rosie, what are you doing here alone in the middle of the night? Let me drive you home. But she starts shouting, 'Leave me alone. It's over. Don't you understand?' I try to take her hand. And then she hits me. That's how I got this," he says and he points at the cut on his face. "That's when I get in my car and drive away."

> 1 Meile entspricht 1,6 Kilometer. Die Briten geben Längen und Entfernungen meist in den traditionellen Maßeinheiten an, obwohl offiziell auch längst das metrische System gilt.

"Where do you go?"

"At first I don't know where to go. I just want to get away. And then I decide to go to my cousin's house for a couple of days. He lives near Lake Grasmere, 14 miles south of here. And then this morning my cousin and I are listening to the breakfast radio show. The reporter says Rosie is dead!"

Dean puts his hand over his eyes.

sample	Probe
fingerprint	Fingerabdruck
to make sense	Sinn ergeben
to get rid of sth.	etw. loswerden

"What do you know about this?" McKenzie asks and puts Rosie's rucksack on the table. "We found it in your garden."

Dean stares at the dirty, pink rucksack with his mouth open.

"Mr Watson, I must ask you to stay here at the station for more questioning. Please give us the name and address of your cousin. We need to check your story. And we also need a DNA sample and your fingerprints."

Exercise 7: Opposites. Wie lautet das Gegenteil der folgenden Adjektive?

1. bored _____
2. alive _____
3. happy _____
4. modern _____

"It looks very bad for Dean," Atkinson says back in the office. "Everything points to him."

"I'm not so sure," McKenzie answers. "It doesn't make sense. Dean says he drove from the stone circle to his cousin in Grasmere. Why did he drive home first and hide the rucksack in his own back garden? Why didn't he throw it in the lake or get rid of it somewhere else on the way to Grasmere?"

"Yes, that was a stupid mistake," Atkinson says. "Maybe Dean went home to get something for the weekend. He panicked and hid the rucksack in his garden."

McKenzie shakes her head.

to panic	in Panik geraten
sharply	*hier:* kritisch, aufmerksam
pie	Pastete
several	mehrere

"Excuse me, Inspector," says Constable Cartwright. "There's a young couple here. They want to talk to you."

"Okay, bring them in," McKenzie answers.

Simon and Wendy walk into the office.

"Oh, hello again, how can we help you?" McKenzie asks.

"I found this near the lake," says Simon nervously and he puts a pink mobile phone on the table.

"It's the dead woman's phone," adds Wendy.

McKenzie looks sharply at them both. "Where exactly did you find this? And when?"

"I found it near our tent yesterday afternoon. I'm sorry that I didn't come here sooner," says Simon. "I didn't know it was important."

"This couple camped near Hawes End Pier Saturday night," McKenzie explains to Atkinson. Then she turns back to Wendy and Simon. "Please go with Constable Cartwright. She will take your fingerprints."

Die Universitätsstadt **Carlisle** hat ca. 75.000 Einwohner und liegt nur 16 Kilometer südlich der Grenze zu Schottland.

Wendy and Simon look shocked. "We aren't suspects, are we?" Wendy asks nervously.

"Don't worry," McKenzie answers. "It's just routine."

Exercise 8: Match up the phrases. Welche der folgenden Begriffe gehören zusammen? Ordnen Sie zu!

1. ☐ get   a) sense
2. ☐ make   b) fingerprints
3. ☐ give   c) rid of
4. ☐ take   d) up

It's lunchtime. McKenzie and Atkinson are sitting in the King's Arms Hotel. Martin Brady is working again and brings them their drinks.

"Would you like something to eat?" he asks.

"Yes please, Martin. I'll have the steak pie," Atkinson says.

"And a chicken salad for me, please," says McKenzie.

When Martin has gone, she puts Rosie's diary on the table. "Listen, she wrote this on Thursday: 'I'm meeting J again this evening in the Royal Scot. I can't wait! He makes me feel so special :-)'. So Dean was right; she had another man."

"The Royal Scot...," Atkinson says. "Sounds like a pub."

"Yes, it's in Carlisle, not far from Rosie's student flat."

She takes a plastic bag with Rosie's phone out of her handbag. "There are several text messages to someone called J. Here's the last one. She sent it late on Saturday night."

Atkinson reads, 'I'm having a terrible time here. Dean doesn't understand it's over. I need to see you, J. Meet me in half an hour at the Castlerigg Stone Circle. Please!'

"I'm going to Carlisle this afternoon," McKenzie says. "I want to find this mysterious J – quickly! But first, I'll send the forensic team to check around the stone circle. Meanwhile, you can question those campers again."

sign	Zeichen
accident	Unfall
to examine	untersuchen
hedge	Hecke
narrow	eng

Exercise 9: Police work quiz. Finden Sie 8 Begriffe zum Thema Polizeiarbeit!

D	E	T	E	S	I	C	O	F	I	L
O	D	N	A	U	M	X	U	R	E	S
I	N	V	E	S	T	I	G	A	T	E
C	S	A	M	P	L	E	D	R	I	T
L	F	O	R	E	N	S	I	C	T	E
U	N	D	I	C	R	I	M	E	R	U
E	N	D	A	T	I	O	N	R	A	L
F	I	N	G	E	R	P	R	I	N	T
S	T	A	N	T	I	O	N	A	L	S

"Things look very bad for you, Dean," Atkinson says later that afternoon in the interview room at Penrith police station. "Our forensic team found signs of a car accident on the road from the town to Castlerigg Stone Circle.

That's where you spoke to Rosie the last time. Plus we **examined** your car. There are scratches on the front and the left side."

"I scratched it on a **hedge** last week," Dean replies. "You know how **narrow** the roads are around here. Everyone has scratches on their cars."

"Dean, you must tell me everything you know. If not, you are only making things worse for yourself."

"All I know is this: Rosie was alive and well when I last saw her," Dean shouts. "You are questioning the wrong man!"

4. The Killer

At 5 o'clock, McKenzie phones. "Hello Atkinson, how are you getting on?"

"Dean still says he's **innocent**. What's your news?"

"I spoke to Rosie's **flatmate**. She says Rosie was nervous about going home last weekend. She wanted to finish with Dean. That's all she could tell me."

innocent	unschuldig
flatmate	Mitbewohnerin
to hang up	*hier*: auflegen
timber-framed	Fachwerk…
customer	Kunde
shelf (*pl* shelves)	Regal

"Where are you now?" Atkinson asks.

"Outside the Royal Scot pub. Maybe someone here can help me to find J. I'll phone you again later." She **hangs up**.

The Royal Scot is an old **timbered-framed** pub in the centre of Carlisle. It's early evening and there are only a few **customers** inside. A barman is putting glasses on the **shelves**.

McKenzie shows him her ID card.

"How can I help you, Inspector?" the barman asks.

"Do you know this young woman? Or the man who is with her?" McKenzie shows him the screensaver on Rosie's phone.

He looks at it carefully.

"Yes, the woman... she's dead, isn't she? I read about it in the newspaper."

"I'm afraid so. Was she a customer here?"

"Yes, she came here quite often in the last few months."

"What about the man?"

"Jessy? He's a regular."

regular	Stammkunde
crowded	überfüllt
to hit the bull's eye	ins Schwarze treffen
to cheer	jubeln
to interrupt	unterbrechen

"Jessy... Do you know his surname or his address?"

"You can ask him yourself. He's playing darts in the next room." The barman points to a door.

McKenzie thanks him and goes into the next room. Here it is much more crowded. A group of men are laughing and drinking beer. A young man with blonde hair and a leather jacket picks up a dart. He throws it at the board on the wall and it hits the bull's eye. The others cheer loudly.

"DI McKenzie, Penrith Police." She has to shout because it is so noisy.

The men turn around and stare at her angrily.

"Sorry to interrupt your game. But I need to talk to Jessy. That's you, isn't it?" she asks the blonde man.

Darts hat sich seit 1900 in den Industriezentren Englands zu einer Freizeitsportart der Arbeiterklasse entwickelt. Er wird meist in Pubs gespielt und der Sieger bekommt als Preis oft eine Runde Bier spendiert!

"What do you want?" he replies coldly.

"It's about Rosie Chapman. You were friends, weren't you?"

"Not really. I met her here a couple of times. That's all."

"Well, Rosie thought you were friends," says McKenzie. "She sent you a text message shortly before she died. She wanted to meet you. Where were you on Saturday night?"
"I was here until closing time. Then I went home."
"And between midnight and 3 a.m.?"
"I was in bed asleep."
"Can anyone **confirm** this?" McKenzie asks.
"No, I was alone," Jessy answers.
Just then McKenzie's phone rings.

> **Exercise 10: Correct the mistakes.** Lesen Sie weiter und korrigieren Sie die 6 Fehler!
>
> "Its Atkinson. Listen, Dean Watson's neighbour Mrs Clarke was hear. She saw something suspicious on Sunday morning around 2 a.m. A car parked outside Deans house. Then anyone got out off the car and she threw somethink into Dean's garden."
>
> 1. _____ 2. _____
> 3. _____ 4. _____
> 5. _____ 6. _____

"She?" McKenzie asks.
"Yes, Mrs Clarke says the person was wearing high heels."
"What kind of car was it?"
"A small car. She thinks it was a Mini."
"**Hang on** a second, Atkinson," McKenzie says and turns to Jessy. "What car do you drive?"

"A Ford pickup," Jessy says. "It's parked outside."
"Okay, I need your full name, address and phone number. I'll speak to you again later. Atkinson, I'm coming right back."

It's 7 p.m. Atkinson parks the car at the Loft Nightclub.
"Look, that's Martin Brady's car over there," he says. "Do you really think a guest from the nightclub threw Rosie's rucksack into Dean's garden?"

to confirm	bestätigen
to hang on	warten
shed	Schuppen
to fetch	holen
sink	Spülbecken

"Yes, I do," McKenzie replies. "Who else drives around Keswick at two o'clock in the morning in high heels! Cartwright is trying to find out if anyone on the list that Martin gave us has a Mini. Maybe Martin remembers something else that could help."
It's not opening time yet, so the front door of the nightclub is still locked.
"The entrance to the kitchen is at the back of the house," Atkinson says. "Maybe Martin is there."
As they walk round the building, they pass a shed.
"Or maybe he's in there fetching more beer. I'll look inside."
"Okay," says McKenzie and she walks towards the kitchen. When she opens the door, she hears loud music and sees Martin washing his hands in the kitchen sink.
"Hello, Mr Brady," she says.
Martin is surprised. "Oh hello, I didn't hear you coming."
He turns off the radio and puts his hands behind his back.

Atkinson opens the door to the shed. It's dark inside, but he can see a pile of beer crates. And there is a strong smell of paint. He moves closer and sees something behind the crates... a red Mini. He kneels down in front of the car and touches it. His finger comes away red. Fresh paint! Behind the Mini, Atkinson sees something else standing under a sheet. He pulls the sheet back and sees a bicycle. The front wheel is broken and the handlebar is scratched.

pile	Stapel
crate	Kiste
to kneel down	sich hinknien
handlebar	Fahrradlenker

Could this be Rosie's bike? I must tell McKenzie at once, he thinks.

Exercise 11: Definitions. Ordnen Sie den Wörtern die passende Definition zu!

1. ☐ to say that sth. is correct   a) to fetch
2. ☐ to end a phone call   b) to confirm
3. ☐ to get sth. and bring it back   c) to hang on
4. ☐ to wait   d) to hang up

In the kitchen, McKenzie is questioning Martin. "Do you remember a Mini parked here on Saturday night?"
Before he can answer, her phone rings. "Excuse me a moment, Martin. Hello, Cartwright?"

"Inspector, I checked the list of names. Annabelle Newton has a red Mini. Her father bought it for her last week."

"Thanks, Cartwright. I'll talk to Annabelle after Martin. Oh! It looks like I can talk to both right now," she adds as she sees Annabelle coming into the kitchen.

startled	erschrocken
to stammer	stottern
to lend sb. sth.	jmd. etw. ausleihen
to arrest sb.	jmd. festnehmen
murder	Mord
doorway	Eingangstür
suddenly	plötzlich

Annabelle looks startled when she sees McKenzie.

"Hello Inspector. How can we help you?" she asks.

"I'm checking the cars at the nightclub on Saturday night," McKenzie replies. "You have a Mini, don't you? Can we take a look at it?"

"It... I... it's not here," stammers Annabelle. "I lent it❶ to my brother. He's… gone away with it on holiday."

"Okay, I have to check that. I'm sure you understand. Can you give me your brother's name and phone number?"

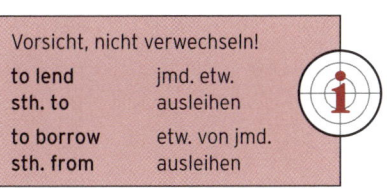

Vorsicht, nicht verwechseln!
| to lend sth. to | jmd. etw. ausleihen |
| to borrow sth. from | etw. von jmd. ausleihen |

Annabelle looks at Martin in panic. He just looks sad. Then she looks wildly at the knives hanging on the kitchen wall.

"Stay where you are. Hands up! I am arresting both of you for the murder of Rosie Chapman!" shouts Atkinson from the doorway.

Now McKenzie is startled. Martin and Annabelle put their hands in the air. There is red paint on Martin's fingers. Suddenly McKenzie understands.

At the police station, Annabelle is crying.

"Martin Brady already told us everything," McKenzie says. "Now we want to hear it from you."

proud	stolz
boot	*hier*: Kofferraum
to tie	(fest)binden
spot	*hier*: Ort
to hate	hassen

Annabelle wipes her eyes and starts to tell her story. "Around 2 a.m., my friends start to leave the party. Martin is cleaning up and I stay to talk to him. He's a really nice man. I like him very much. We have a couple of drinks together. And then I have a crazy idea. I say, come on, Martin. Let's drive up to the stone circle. There's a full moon tonight. It's romantic! He says okay. He wants to drive. But I say, no. Let me take you in my new car! It's a present from my Dad. He's so proud because I am going to university." She wipes her eyes again.

"Please go on," McKenzie says.

"We drive along the narrow road. And then, as we are going around a corner, there's a loud noise. The car hits something. Martin and I jump out to look. And I see her... it's Rosie. She's lying on the road. I run to her and I want to help her. But it's too late. She is… she's dead."

Annabelle puts her head in her hands.

"What happens next?" McKenzie asks her.

"I start to cry. My friend is dead and my life is ruined. How can I become a doctor now? Martin puts his arm around my shoulder. He says, 'We can't help Rosie now,

False friends
Das Verb **to become** bedeutet *werden* und nicht *bekommen*.

but we *can* help you.' So we put Rosie and her rucksack in the boot of the car. Then we tie the bike to the back of the Mini and we drive to a lonely spot at the lake."

"Hawes End?" Atkinson asks.

"Yes, that's right. Martin throws Rosie into the water. He wants to throw the rucksack and the bike in, too. But just then, I see someone coming with a torch, so we start running. I'm so scared – and I drop the rucksack. When I pick it up, something falls out. But there is no time to look for it.

On the way back to the Loft, we pass Dean's house. Martin hates Dean, you know. He's always so aggressive. 'Stop the car,' says Martin. 'Everyone knows that Dean shouted at Rosie. They will think that *he* killed her.' So I get out of the car and quickly throw the rucksack into Dean's garden. After that we drive to the Loft. Martin says, 'I'll hide the bike and the car in the shed until we have a better idea.' But the next day the town is already full of police, so we can't do anything else."

Exercise 12: True or false? Welche Aussagen sind korrekt? Markieren Sie mit richtig ✔ oder falsch – !

1. Martin threw the rucksack into Dean's garden. ☐
2. Annabelle's car hit Rosie's car. ☐
3. Annabelle wanted to be a doctor. ☐
4. Martin wanted to help Annabelle. ☐

The interview with Annabelle is over. She is crying when two police officers take her away in handcuffs.

"So it wasn't murder. Just a terrible accident," Atkinson says. "It's a very sad story."

"Yes, it is," McKenzie agrees. "But I'm glad we solved the case. Now life can get back to normal at Derwentwater."

handcuffs *pl*	Handschellen
to solve	lösen
case	*hier:* Fall

Exercise 13: Verb forms. Wie lauten das Present Simple und Past Simple der folgenden Verben in der dritten Person?

1. to notice — *notices* — *noticed*
2. to be — _____ — _____
3. to solve — _____ — _____
4. to say — _____ — _____
5. to have — _____ — _____
6. to cry — _____ — _____

Deadly Duet

Oliver Astley

 Football Legends

Detective Inspector Carol Blackwater is on holiday. After a week in France, she is back in Scotland. Her house is in Renfrewshire, twenty minutes away from Glasgow. She is going back to work in the city tomorrow morning. Today, she is relaxing at home.

She turns on the television and sees two tall, athletic men. They both have short, grey hair. One man has strong shoulders. The other one is very thin.

Detective Inspector (DI)	Kriminalkommissarin
island	Insel
sunglasses *pl*	Sonnenbrille
annoying	lästig

It's Hunter and Lamb again, she thinks. They're always on TV these days. Are they going to sing their song again? She hopes not. She hears that song every hour when the radio's on. Her two boys are always singing it around the house.

The studio looks like a tropical island. Hunter and Lamb are wearing sombreros, large sunglasses and colourful Hawaiian shirts. They each pick up a red football. Then they look at each other and the music begins.

"How annoying!" Carol says to herself.

She wants to turn off the television, but at that moment her younger son runs into the living room.

"Yippee!" he shouts and starts singing with the two men.

Hunter and Lamb are now dancing very badly. It's always the same routine, thinks Carol. Loud music, **loud** shirts, no musical talent.

loud	*hier*: grell
smash hit	Superhit
retired	in Rente
striker	Stürmer
wife	Ehefrau
capital	*hier*: Hauptstadt
rivals *pl*	Gegner

She leaves the room to make sandwiches for lunch, but she can still hear this summer's **smash hit**, "A Funny Old Game". Roy Hunter and Billy Lamb are **retired** footballers. They are now over fifty years old. When they were younger, they both played for the English national team. But they are not good friends. Hunter is from the North and was a **striker** for Liverpool. He now lives with his **wife** in a large house in Glasgow. Carol sometimes sees him in the city. Lamb is from London. He was a striker for Arsenal and still lives in the **capital** with his family. Liverpool and Arsenal are big **rivals**, and so were the two strikers. For many people, it is bizarre to see them singing and dancing together now – but it is also very funny.

"Lunch is ready!" says Carol. "Come and get it!"

Exercise 1: True or false? Welche Aussagen sind korrekt? Markieren Sie mit richtig ✔ oder falsch – !

1. Carol Blackwater has two sons. ❐
2. Roy Hunter and Billy Lamb are good friends. ❐
3. Arsenal is a football club in London. ❐
4. Hunter and Lamb are very good at singing. ❐

The two men stop dancing and the music ends.

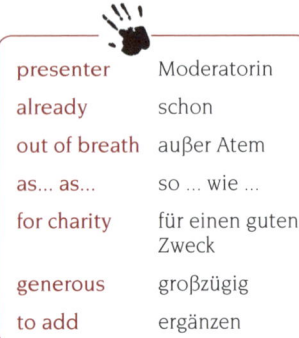

presenter	Moderatorin
already	schon
out of breath	außer Atem
as... as...	so ... wie ...
for charity	für einen guten Zweck
generous	großzügig
to add	ergänzen

"Brilliant! Great fun!" says Jenny Green, the television **presenter**, live from central London. "Please download the song 'A Funny Old Game' to help Hunter and Lamb. Is it doing well, gentlemen?"

"Yes, we **already** have over a million pounds!" says Lamb enthusiastically. He is a little **out of breath**. "It's fantastic, but please send **as** much money **as** you can. It's all **for charity**. We want more children in Africa to enjoy a healthy life and play football."

"What's your goal?" asks Jenny Green.

The two men have the same conversation in every studio that they visit. Lamb lets Hunter answer.

"Well, we are already over our goal of five hundred thousand pounds. People are very **generous**. At the moment, we have more than a million pounds to help football teams and schools in Africa. We can pay for lots of trainers to work over there."

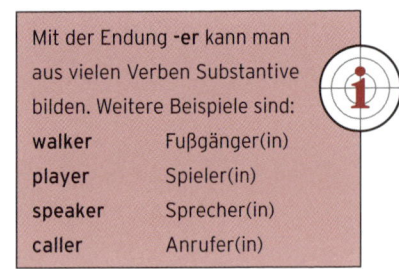

Mit der Endung **-er** kann man aus vielen Verben Substantive bilden. Weitere Beispiele sind:

walker	Fußgänger(in)
player	Spieler(in)
speaker	Sprecher(in)
caller	Anrufer(in)

"I don't know why they like to hear us sing," Lamb **adds** and smiles into the camera. "They should pay us to keep quiet!"

Exercise 2: Fill in the blanks. Lesen Sie weiter und ergänzen Sie den Text mit den fehlenden Wörtern!

| hand | young | Who's | boy | name | What's |

"Wonderful!" the presenter laughs. "And now we have some questions from our **viewers**. "Who's first? What's your **1.** _____ and where do you come from?"

"Hi!" says a **2.** _____ boy. "I'm Robert from Derby."

"Hello, Robert," the two footballers say together.

"**3.** _____ your question, Robert?" asks Jenny.

"**4.** _____ better at football?" the young boy asks.

Hunter and Lamb smile. At the same time, they lift up one **5.** _____, **point to** their own **chests** and say, "Me!"

"Can I have your **autograph**?" the **6.** _____ continues.

"Yes, of course," says Jenny. "Don't **hang up**. Who's next? Hello?"

"Er, hello."

"Hello, caller!" **repeats** Jenny. "What's your name and where do you come from?"

viewers *pl*	Zuschauer
to point (to)	zeigen (auf)
chest	Brust
autograph	Autogramm
to hang up	*hier*: auflegen
to repeat	wiederholen

"It's, uh, Gareth. Gareth from Paisley in Renfrewshire," the man says in a slow, deep **voice**.

"Hello, Gareth!" Lamb says.

"Hello, Gareth," Hunter repeats a second later.

There's something about Gareth's voice that he doesn't like. His words are not very clear, and he definitely isn't Scottish.

"And what's your question, Gareth?" asks Jenny with a smile.

There is no answer.

"Are you there, Gareth? Can you hear me?" Jenny continues.

"Er… yeah. Do you want to die, Hunter?" The man's voice

voice	Stimme
drunk	betrunken
to pay sb. back	es jmd. heimzahlen
producer	Produzent
prank call	Telefonstreich

is now faster, louder and more aggressive. He sounds **drunk**.

"I'm sorry?" says Jenny. "What did you say?"

"I asked Hunter if he wants to die. I'm going to **pay him back** for what he did. I'm going to kill you, Hunter! You–"

The call ends. Hunter and Lamb are looking at each other in shock. Jenny can hear the **producer** in her ear. He is telling her to continue the interview.

"I'm so sorry, gentlemen," she says. "A **prank call**, I'm sure."

Hunter stands up and takes off his microphone. "I'm not going to sit here and listen to this," he says.

"Sit down, Roy!" Lamb shouts.

Hunter does not listen, so Lamb also stands up and takes off his microphone. Both men walk out of the studio.

"Oh dear!" says Jenny. "Let's go to a commercial break. I'm sorry, viewers. We'll be back in three minutes."

Oh dear!	Oh je!
commercial break	Werbepause
strange	seltsam

Exercise 3: Word search. Finden Sie die versteckten Wörter und ordnen Sie sie den Übersetzungen zu!

A	S	T	R	U	K	E	I	V	A
L	V	Y	G	D	N	A	L	I	S
R	O	L	E	V	O	I	C	E	I
E	C	I	S	L	A	N	D	W	L
A	E	I	D	R	U	T	I	E	L
D	A	S	T	R	I	K	E	R	Y
Y	G	E	N	E	R	O	U	S	O
O	B	A	N	N	O	Y	I	N	G

1. schon _____
2. albern _____
3. Stürmer _____
4. großzügig _____
5. Zuschauer _____
6. Insel _____
7. lästig _____
8. Stimme _____

Back in Scotland, DI Carol Blackwater is watching television with her two sons. They are still eating their sandwiches. "That was very strange, wasn't it?" she asks them.

"I'm going to kill you, Hunter!" the older boy says. He points his finger like a pistol.
"Bang! Bang!"
"Oh, no!" his brother **cries out**.
The younger boy drops his plate.

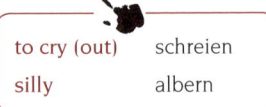

| to cry (out) | schreien |
| silly | albern |

He falls to the floor with his hands on his chest. He closes his eyes and sticks out his tongue.

"Don't be **silly**," their mother says. "I see enough dead people at work. I don't want any more in the house."

# A Bitter Breakfast

Early the next morning, Roy Hunter and Billy Lamb are visiting another studio. They are in Manchester.

"I'm getting too old for this," says Lamb.

"I hate breakfast television, too," agrees Hunter. "We're only here because it's on the way to Glasgow. Saturday night TV is always much better! We'll have a good time doing that this evening. After that, I'll be at home all week. Thank god!"

to agree	zustimmen
to yawn	gähnen
to see the point	den Sinn verstehen

The two men sit down on a large, red sofa. Lamb feels small next to Hunter. In front of them there is a glass table with tea, fruit juice and some biscuits. Hunter yawns loudly and looks at his watch.

"It's before eight o'clock. I should still be in bed," he says.

Achten Sie bei englischen Wendungen besonders auf Präpositionen. Man verwendet sie oft anders als im Deutschen:
at home zu Hause
home das Zuhause; nach Hause
I'm going home.
Ich gehe nach Hause.
He wasn't at home last night.
Er war gestern Abend nicht zu Hause.

Lamb is not listening. He is looking at his phone.

"It was your idea to do all these interviews," Hunter continues. "I don't see the point."

Lamb is silent for a few seconds, then he shows Hunter a website.

"Look. Our video has more than five hundred million hits in less than a month! That's a lot of money."

"Yes, but we're not helping by being on television."

"It's in our contract with the music company. Anyway, it's mainly younger people who use those websites. People our age mostly watch TV."

Hunter closes his eyes and breathes out heavily through his large, round nose.

"Don't do that!" Lamb says in a loud, angry voice. "I hate it when you do that!"

Hunter opens one eye and smiles a little. He inhales and starts to breathe out slowly through his nose again.

"Ugh! I'm going to the toilet," says Lamb.

He stands up and leaves his phone on the sofa. When he is out of the room, Hunter picks up the phone. He reads some of his partner's messages and emails.

hit	*hier*: Klick
contract	Vertrag
anyway	jedenfalls
to breathe out heavily	tief ausatmen
to embarrass	blamieren
Police Constable (PC)	Polizist
death threat	Morddrohung
seriously	ernst
probably	wahrscheinlich
lie	Lüge
ago	vor

"Billy, Billy, Billy," he says to himself.

He then opens the photo gallery and looks at all the different pictures. Some are from parties, others from sports events and even romantic holidays.

I can embarrass Lamb with some of this on live television, Hunter thinks. He laughs at the idea.

Exercise 4: Choose the correct alternative. Lesen Sie weiter und wählen Sie die richtige Verbform!

In Westminster, the heart of London, **Police Constable** Ajit Mulla **1.** is analysing / analyses yesterday's phone call to Roy Hunter on live television. He **2.** have / has all the material from the studio.

"It **3.** is / are a **death threat** to a celebrity," he explains to a small group of officers by the coffee machine. "We always **4.** taking / take these things very **seriously**, but it was **probably** just a prank call – someone who **5.** wants / is wanting to feel important."

PC Mulla walks back to his desk. The man called himself Gareth. That is probably a lie, Mulla thinks. But it is true that this "Gareth" is – or was – in Renfrewshire. The call came from a phone box in Paisley, just outside Glasgow. Maybe someone saw him make the call? Very few people use phone boxes these days.

Back in Manchester, Hunter and Lamb are at the end of their last morning interview of the week.

"I have one final question," the presenter says. "As our older viewers will know, you two were legendary rivals twenty years ago. Are you friends now?"

Die Futur drückt hier Gewissheit aus: „Wie unsere älteren Zuschauer sicher wissen, ..."

"Of course!" Hunter answers with a laugh. "We tell each other everything. For example, Billy was at a **topless bar** last night. He loves the women up here. That's why he's really in Manchester, you know."

topless bar	Oben-ohne-Bar
to reply	antworten
to thump	(mit der Faust) schlagen
lazy	faul

Lamb's face begins to turn red behind his thin, grey beard. "Don't be silly," he says.

"People saw you there," Hunter smiles.

"You're an idiot," Lamb **replies** angrily.

"Thank you, gentlemen," the presenter says. "I think we can see how much you like each other."

Hunter grins at Lamb and **thumps** him lightly on the arm while the presenter says goodbye to the viewers. Lamb instinctively thumps Hunter back a little harder.

After the lights go out, the two football stars leave the studio and get into a long, black limousine. Lamb is not talking to Hunter. He is still angry. The two men often say silly things in their interviews, but Hunter went too far today. Hunter takes out his phone. He has a voicemail message from a PC Mulla of the London Metropolitan Police.

"I'm sure you know that people say all sorts of things and don't really mean them," Hunter repeats the message with a strong London accent. "Huh! The police are so **lazy**!"

"Well, he's right," Lamb says. "Just think about what fans shout at football matches!"

"Hmph!"

"And all those comments below our video on the Internet? You can't take them seriously."

Exercise 5: Translation quiz. Übersetzen Sie die Wörter ins Englische und enträtseln Sie das Lösungswort!

1. Lüge
2. Vertrag
3. blamieren
4. antworten
5. tief (ausatmen)
6. ernst
7. zustimmen
8. gähnen

Hidden word: _ _ _ _ _ _ _ _

"What do you mean? What do they say?" asks Hunter. "I never look at that website."

"See for yourself," Lamb says. "It's a long drive to Glasgow, and I have nothing to say to you."

Hunter opens their webpage and begins reading.

This isn't too bad, he thinks. A lot of people say how wonderful the song is and how funny the two men are. Then he sees some strange comments. They are all about him, not Lamb or the music.

"Hunter took everything from me. I'm going to make him pay," he reads aloud. "Who could that be, Billy?"

"You tell me," says Lamb.

 Saturday Night Death

Alasdair McCoy is smiling into the camera. The young presenter is wearing an expensive blue jacket and a white shirt with no tie.

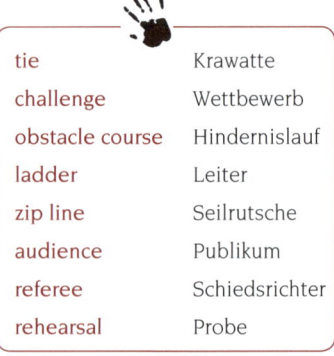

tie	Krawatte
challenge	Wettbewerb
obstacle course	Hindernislauf
ladder	Leiter
zip line	Seilrutsche
audience	Publikum
referee	Schiedsrichter
rehearsal	Probe

"Hello and welcome to part three of 'Celebrity Challenge', live from the sunny city of Glasgow!"

The presenter is standing between Roy Hunter and Billy Lamb. They are wearing their sombreros and Hawaiian shirts again.

"This is a fantastic game for two sports rivals!" says Alasdair. "The winner is the first to finish."

The three men are at the starting line of a short obstacle course.

"You can see what to do," the presenter continues. "Run along the planks without falling off, then jump over the pool of water. After that, climb all the way up the ladder and go down the zip line. At the end, kick three balls into the goal."

"Okay, I'm ready," says Hunter without enthusiasm.

"I hope you're not too old for this," the presenter laughs.

"Old? We're faster than you!" Lamb replies with a smile.

"Really?" asks Alasdair. He thinks this is funny. "What do you think, audience, is he faster than me?"

> Mit **Good luck** wünscht man jemandem Viel Glück. "Glück haben" übersetzt man mit **to be lucky**, "glücklich sein" aber mit **to be happy**.

There is a loud "no" from the people in the studio.

"Oh, yes I am!" says Lamb. "Do you think you can win against me?"

"Let's make it more interesting," the presenter says and takes off his jacket. "Roy, you can be the referee!"

"Hah, fine. Good luck, Lamb!" Hunter smiles.

He is happy that Alasdair is doing the challenge. Lamb is quite fast for an older man. He won every time in rehearsal. Hopefully, he won't lose now on live television!

A loud voice fills the studio: "Three… two… one… go!" Dramatic music begins to play.

Exercise 6: Unscramble. Lesen Sie weiter und bilden Sie Wörter aus dem Buchstabenchaos!

Lamb and McCoy run across the 1. klanps _____ at the same time and jump into the air. McCoy lands on the other side of the 2. rawet _____, but Lamb jumped too 3. yelar _____. He is holding on to the side of the pool with his 4. gels _____ in the water.

The **5. acedniue** _____ are shouting and applauding.

"Go on, Lamb!" Hunter calls. "Keep moving!"

Lamb quickly climbs out of the pool and begins to pull himself up one of the two ladders. He looks up and sees that McCoy is already near the top. How did he get there so fast?

Hunter runs to the bottom of the zip line. It is difficult to see what is happening because of the studio lights. There is someone at the top of the ladder. A second later, a loud gasp fills the air.

gasp	hörbares Einatmen
rude word	Schimpfwort
inflatable cushion	aufblasbare Matte
short	*hier*: klein
curly	lockig

Lamb sees McCoy falling and hears him shouting a rude word. Then he hears Hunter's voice from below.

"Stop! Help! Stop the music!"

Alasdair McCoy is lying on his back. A line of blood is coming out of his nose. The inflatable cushion below him has no air in it.

Less than an hour later, a short woman with curly, red hair meets Hunter and Lamb in the television studio. She has bright green eyes, black glasses and a thin smile.

"Hello, gentlemen. I'm Detective Inspector Carol Blackwater. Can you tell me what happened here tonight?"

Lamb's face is white. He is still in shock.

to take sb.'s place	an jds Stelle treten
to look into	untersuchen
to reach	erreichen

"What happened?" repeats Hunter. "I'll tell you what happened! Someone tried to kill me! Now Alasdair McCoy is in hospital because he took my place."

"Someone tried to kill you?" asks the inspector. "Are you talking about that phone call yesterday?"

"Yes, someone wants me dead!" says Hunter.

"Hmm, I saw that with my sons," says DI Blackwater. "Wasn't it just a prank call? We heard from the police in London, and they–"

"No, and it's not only the call," Hunter replies quickly in a bitter voice. "There are all kinds of comments about me below our video online."

"We'll look into that," says DI Blackwater, "although people do write strange things on the Internet. You can't take it all to heart."

Das Hilfsverb **to do** dient manchmal dazu, eine Handlung zu betonen. Es kommt oft in Verbindung mit **but** vor: *I do want to meet your friend, but I have no time today.*

"I know, I know," Hunter says.

The inspector walks slowly along the obstacle course with the show's producer, who is very nervous, and the two ex-footballers. Lamb is very quiet.

"Well, Alasdair reaches the top of that ladder on the left – and then he just falls!" the producer explains. "It looks as if there was a problem with the ladder."

"A problem?" DI Blackwater asks. "What kind of problem?"

Exercise 7: Match up the words. Welche Wortpaare gehören zusammen? Ordnen Sie zu!

1. ☐ phone   a) course
2. ☐ rude   b) lights
3. ☐ obstacle   c) call
4. ☐ studio   d) word

"There's oil on it… lots of oil. We have no idea why. The set team don't know anything about it."

The inspector stops taking notes and makes eye contact with each of the three men. The producer does not know what else to say. Lamb is shaking his head slowly with one hand on his thin beard. Hunter is clearly angry.

"We'll do some tests on the oil," explains DI Blackwater. "I need the name of everyone who was here today – workers and visitors. I also want all the recordings you have."

"Yes, of course," says the producer.

Hunter is kicking some cushions and mats on the studio floor.

"Hey, why isn't there any air in this?" he asks.

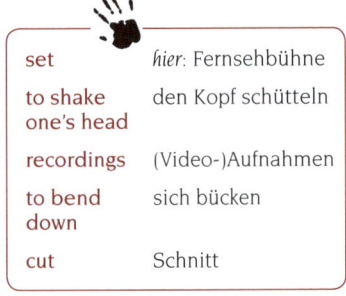

set	*hier*: Fernsehbühne
to shake one's head	den Kopf schütteln
recordings	(Video-)Aufnahmen
to bend down	sich bücken
cut	Schnitt

DI Blackwater bends down and looks at the inflatable cushion. "There's a cut in the material here, can you see?"

"That's very strange," the producer says.

Just then, the inspector's phone rings. She stands up and turns her back to the three men.

"Yes… I understand," she says in a quiet voice. "When was that? … Nine twenty. Is his family at the hospital?"

She hangs up a few moments later and bites her lip.

"Bad news?" asks Hunter.

"Yes. Alasdair McCoy is dead."

Exercise 8: Odd one out. Welches Wort ist das „schwarze Schaf"? Unterstreichen Sie das Wort, das nicht in die Reihe passt!

1. presenter   studio   audience   cushion
2. chest   ball   shoulder   knee
3. to yawn   to agree   to reply   to say
4. heavily   silly   seriously   badly

Trouble for Hunter

A little after ten o'clock on Monday morning, DI Blackwater arrives at the Hunters' large house in the west end of Glasgow. There are three expensive cars in the middle of the long **drive**. The one nearest the road is a new Italian sports car. The front door opens before she reaches it.

trouble	Problem(e)
drive	*hier*: Auffahrt
What took you so long?	Wo sind Sie so lange geblieben?
safe	sicher
almost	fast
to succeed	Erfolg haben, erfolgreich sein

"Ah, Inspector! **What took you so long?**" asks Roy aggressively. "I tried to call you a hundred times yesterday."

"Good morning, Mr Hunter," she replies. "I'm very sorry, but we have a lot of work at the station. I came as quickly as I could."

"Listen," Roy begins, "my wife and I don't feel **safe**. Someone's trying to kill me, and on Saturday they **almost succeeded**. As you know, we stayed in a hotel for two nights. But we're not going to live like that forever. This

> **Lerntipp**
> Versuchen Sie bei neuen Vokabeln gleich verwandte Wörter mit zu lernen. Durch solche Wortfamilien vergrößert sich Ihr Wortschatz sehr schnell, hier z.B.:
>
> | | |
> |---|---|
> | **to succeed** | Erfolg haben, erfolgreich sein |
> | **success** | Erfolg |
> | **successfully** | erfolgreich |

is our home. We want you to pro-tect us!"

"Can I come in?" the inspector asks. "We have a lot to talk about." Without speaking, Roy holds

to protect	schützen
concerned	besorgt
accident	Unfall
evidence	Hinweise, Beweis(e)

open the door and lets DI Blackwater inside. They enter the living room and sit down.

"Hello, Inspector. I'm Megan Hunter, Roy's wife. Thank you so much for coming."

Exercise 9: Spelling mistakes. Lesen Sie weiter, unterstreichen Sie die sechs Schreibfehler und verbessern Sie sie!

"You must both be very concerned," the inspektor begins. "I want to let you know that we're working extremly hard to find out what happened on Saturday night."
"Are you? I hope you're asking the peeple who work at that studio," says Roy.
"Yes, I know what your thinking," DI Blackwater explains. "Perhaps the person who put oil on the ladder also let the air out of the inflatable cushion? But maybe both thinks were just an accident. We're still analysing all the evidence. It's our job to think about every thing."

1. _____ 2. _____
3. _____ 4. _____
5. _____ 6. _____

"An accident?!" repeats Roy. "Hah! You can't be serious."
Megan puts a hand on her **husband's** shoulder.
"Listen to the inspector, dear," she says. "I'm sure she'll keep us safe."
"Mr and Mrs Hunter," DI Blackwater continues, "is there anyone out there who wants to **hurt you**?"

husband	Ehemann
to hurt sb.	jmd. verletzen
to go off	*hier:* losgehen
broken	kaputt, gebrochen
about	*hier:* circa

"No, I'm everyone's friend," Roy says bitterly. "Even the little children in Africa love me."
"Well, I don't think Billy Lamb likes you very much at the moment," Megan says. "You embarrassed him on television with that story about the topless bar."
"What?" asks the inspector.
"It's nothing," says Roy. "Forget about it. And forget about Lamb. He's back in London now."
At that moment, a loud siren **goes off**.
"That's your car alarm, Roy!" says Megan.
Roy jumps from his chair and looks out of the front window.
"My new car!" he shouts. "One of the windows is **broken**!"
Roy runs out of the front door. DI Blackwater tells Megan to stay where she is and quickly follows him outside.
"Mr Hunter, stop!" she shouts.
Roy is already running towards his Italian sports car. It's parked **about** thirty metres from the house. He is running very quickly and cannot see what the two women can see from the front door: smoke!

"Mr Hunter! Stop!" repeats DI Blackwater.

"What is it?" he calls back.

"Can you—"

Suddenly there is a loud explosion.

"Roy!!"

Megan puts her hands over her mouth and falls to her knees. DI Blackwater bends down and places her arms around the woman's shoulders. The inspector's **ears are ringing**. She can't hear anything. She looks up to find Hunter. But all that she can see is fire and thick, black smoke.

suddenly	plötzlich
sb.'s ears are ringing	jmd. klingen die Ohren
to notice	bemerken
⚡ Damn!	Verdammt!
fire engine	Feuerwehrauto
ambulance	Krankenwagen
shaken	*hier*: erschüttert
to count oneself lucky	sich glücklich schätzen

Then DI Blackwater **notices** someone at the bottom of the drive. It is a short, fat man in a hat and sunglasses. He turns around quickly and walks away.

Damn, she thinks, who's that man? She wants to follow him, but Hunter needs help…

Minutes later, a **fire engine**, **ambulance** and three police cars are at the Hunters' house. There are men and women in uniform everywhere.

Megan is next to her husband. She is holding his hand. Roy is **shaken**, but the explosion did not hurt him too badly.

"He can **count himself lucky**," says DI Blackwater. "This was no accident."

"Thank god you're okay!" Megan repeats again and again.

"You're not safe here," the inspector continues. "We're going to send two police officers with you to the hospital. After that, I want you to stay at a hotel. We'll protect you, of course."

"But this is our home!" says Megan with tears in her eyes.

"Yes, I understand, but your home is now a crime scene. We need to find whoever did this!"

Exercise 10: Definitions. Welches Wort aus dem vorangehenden Textabschnitt wird erklärt?

1. an opening covered with glass   _____
2. a very short period of time   _____
3. flames, light and heat   _____
4. a person you know and like   _____

A short time later, a tall fireman walks up to DI Blackwater. He is holding a piece of glass in his left hand.

"A petrol bomb," he says seriously. "I think that's what caused the explosion."

"Thanks, Calum," the inspector replies. "Now tell me who threw it – and I'll buy you a beer."

The fireman slowly takes off his helmet and holds it under one arm. "I can't tell you that," he says, "but there are CCTV cameras on practically every street in this part of the city. The person who did it will be on the recordings."

crime scene	Tatort
to cause	verursachen
CCTV camera	Überwachungskamera

"Hmm, that's one more job for my team. I really need more people there. Everyone is still looking at all the material from 'Celebrity Challenge'."

to remember	sich erinnern
investigation	Ermittlung
to believe	glauben
that reminds me…	wobei mir einfällt …
to be supposed to	sollen

"The TV show? Oh, yes, I remember! How's the investigation going? There was a death threat before all of this happened, wasn't there?"

"Yes, against Roy Hunter. But it was Alasdair McCoy who died. It's tragic. His parents can't believe it. They are in shock. And the death threat? Well, the police in London sent us a lot of information about the call. We even have an analysis of the caller's voice. Oh, that reminds me…!"

"What?" asks Calum.

"The call came from a phone box in Paisley. We are supposed to find out who it was. I forgot all about it! There was so much to do when I came back from holiday."

"That's not like you, Carol!"

Exercise 11: Phrasal verbs. Was bedeuten folgende Verbausdrücke? Ordnen Sie zu!

1. ☐ to look into   **a)** to return
2. ☐ to hang up   **b)** to investigate
3. ☐ to take off   **c)** to end a call
4. ☐ to come back   **d)** to remove (clothes)

 On the Run

The team of officers at Glasgow police station have a lot to do on Monday. DI Blackwater works until late in the evening.

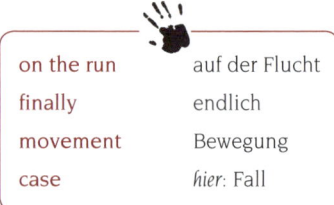

on the run	auf der Flucht
finally	endlich
movement	Bewegung
case	*hier*: Fall

Finally she finds some CCTV recordings of the short, fat man who was outside the Hunters' house. She asks an officer to follow his **movements** through the city. Before she goes home, at 10:30 p.m., she visits the computer specialist for an update.

"Any news, Vikram?"

A young man with large glasses and a bright smile rolls across the room on his office chair.

"Yes, I'm looking at all of the comments on Roy Hunter's social media sites right now," he explains. "There are a few trolls, and three of the accounts are linked."

"Trolls?" asks the inspector.

"Yes, you know… people who make strange and silly comments online. Or the same person in this case."

"Aha. And how do you know it's the same person?"

> „Trolle" nennt man im Internetjargon Foren-Teilnehmer, die absichtlich Schaden anrichten oder Diskussionen steuern wollen, indem sie destruktive und provokante Beiträge erstellen.

"There's a record of the IP addresses. Whoever wrote these things used the Internet café in the science museum."

That's interesting, thinks DI Blackwater. The Glasgow Science Centre is right next to the TV studios on the river – the place where they film "Celebrity Challenge".

backwards	rückwärts
⚡ scum	Abschaum
to regret	bereuen

"What kind of comments?" she asks. "Are any of them serious?"

"Let's see… There are more than forty posts from the user 'YorRentuh'. That's 'Roy Hunter' backwards. Someone made that account last month just to talk about him. There are comments like: 'Hunter is scum. Why doesn't he give his millions of pounds to the Africans?'"

"Hmm, what else?" asks DI Blackwater.

"There are more threats, too. Some of them are from a different user. One message from Friday night even says, 'If Hunter comes back to Glasgow this week, he will regret it!'"

"Oh! Does that user have anything else online?"

Vikram rolls back to the computer and clicks the mouse a few times. He reads the user's profile and interests.

"This says that he's a fifty-four-year-old man. He likes music and sport. And he's a big fan of English football[i] – Liverpool is his team. He also likes reading articles about food and drink."

England, Schottland, Wales und Nordirland haben jeweils eine eigene Fußballliga.

"That profile reminds me of Hunter and Lamb!" DI Blackwater tells Vikram. "Is one of them the user?"

"No, that's **impossible**," Vikram explains. "Remember? We know they were in London on Friday. That's when someone here in Glasgow posted these comments and called the studio."

"Of course. Sorry, I'm so tired; I can't concentrate," says the inspector.

impossible	unmöglich
to act	eingreifen, handeln
to catch	fangen

"Do you believe this person is using the same accounts anywhere else? Perhaps at home or in an office?"

"I can check, but it'll take a few hours. Go home and sleep. I'll email you what I find out."

Exercise 12: Prepositions. Lesen Sie weiter und wählen Sie die richtige Präposition!

Late 1. at / on Tuesday morning, DI Blackwater visits Roy Hunter 2. in / on hospital. He is sitting 3. up / down in bed with a few cuts 4. in / on his hands and face. Megan is still by his side. To protect them both, a police officer 5. in / with uniform is standing 6. over / by the door.

"Do you finally believe that someone wants to kill me, Inspector?" Roy asks angrily.

"I'm sorry we didn't **act** sooner," DI Blackwater says. "We're now doing our best to **catch** the man who did this. What does the name Philipp Jackson mean to you?"

Roy opens his eyes wide. His wife lets out a gasp in shock.

"That idiot?" asks Roy. "He was my manager!"

"Why do you think it's him?" asks Megan. "Philipp stopped working for Roy about fifteen years ago."

"Well, I looked into his past. And we have a lot of evidence – computer records, CCTV recordings and a voice analysis. Do you remember 'Gareth' from Paisley, who threatened you on Friday? We believe that was Philipp Jackson, too."

DI Blackwater pauses so that the Hunters can absorb the news.

"I knew there was something I didn't like about that voice!" Roy begins. "Philipp was my manager after I stopped playing football. He found a few

to absorb	aufnehmen
useless	nichtsnutzig
to fire sb.	jmd. feuern
either	*hier*: auch nicht
to arrest	verhaften

jobs in the media for me, but the man was a useless alcoholic. I never saw him again after I fired him."

"Yes, that was the start of many problems," explains the inspector. "Jackson had trouble getting a new job and he lost his house. I believe that he thinks you caused all his problems. Maybe 'A Funny Old Game' made him remember the past."

"And where is he now?" Roy asks.

DI Blackwater begins to clean her glasses. "We… we can't find him," she says slowly. "He isn't at home or at work today. Nobody saw him yesterday, either. He's an assistant at a television company here in the city – the same one that makes 'Celebrity Challenge'."

"So what are you waiting for?" Roy asks. "Catch him! Arrest him!"

Exercise 13: Opposites. Wie lautet das Gegenteil der folgenden Begriffe im vorangehenden Textabschnitt?

1. quickly _____
2. to continue _____
3. to do nothing _____
4. helpful _____
5. to forget _____
6. end _____

It is late on Tuesday evening. Inside The Black Horse, a small pub in Aberdeen, a group of football fans are standing at the bar. The only other customer is Philipp Jackson. He is sitting next to a very large suitcase.

"Last orders, please!" the barman shouts.

Philipp slowly walks up to the bar and asks for another beer and a whisky. He is already very drunk.

"Don't you think it's time to go home?" the barman asks.

"No, I'm waiting for a ferry," he replies. "I came up from Glasgow this afternoon."

"Ah, that's a long journey. Four pounds eighty, please."

Philipp takes a roll of banknotes from his coat pocket.

"Erm, we don't accept fifties," the barman says. "A credit card is fine. But you have to spend over five pounds."

> Ein 50-Pfund-Schein. Die 5- und 10-Pfund-Scheine nennt man oft *fivers* und *tenners*, wobei der 20-Pfund-Schein *a twenty* heißt.

"Okay, give me some nuts, too. Here's my card."

Philipp looks over his shoulder. There is a television on the wall. A man on the news is talking to DI Blackwater about the death of Alasdair McCoy and the explosion at Roy Hunter's house.

"Oh, **shut up!**" says Philipp. "We don't want more news about that idiot Hunter." He turns back to the bar.

"Hey, Hunter's a good man!" one of the fans replies.

"No, he's not! He's a **back-stabbing** Judas. He took everything I had – my job, my home, my money…!"

customer	Kunde
last orders *pl*	letzte Runde
ferry	Fähre
journey	Reise
to spend	*hier*: ausgeben
⚡ Shut up!	Halt die Klappe!
back-stabbing	hinterhältig
Hands off!	Finger weg!

The football fans ignore him. At that moment, Philipp's face comes on the television screen with a phone number. The barman is the only person who notices. He looks at the suitcase in the corner of the room and reads the name on the credit card in his hand. God, it's the man the police are looking for! he thinks. He must be on the run!

Philipp pays and goes back to his table.

"Hey, boys!" the barman says quietly to the football fans. "Can you stay for another twenty minutes?"

Just after eleven o'clock, Philipp sees the blue lights of two police cars through the window and jumps up. Two strong men quickly move from the bar and put their hands on the fat man's shoulders.

"I don't need your help!" says Philipp. "**Hands off!**"

"You're not going anywhere, Jackson," says the barman.
Two officers in uniform open the door and walk up to the bar. Philipp panics. He throws his beer over the man on his left and tries to run to the back of the pub. But two more football fans stop him.
"Are you trying to run away, Mr Jackson?" asks one of the officers. "Please don't. The police down in Glasgow want to ask you some questions."
"It was all an accident!" says Philipp. "I didn't want to hurt anyone!"
"Save your stories for DI Blackwater!"

Exercise 14: Idioms. Wie lauten die Redewendungen auf Englisch? Übersetzen Sie!

1. Letzte Runde! _____
2. Halt die Klappe! _____
3. Finger weg! _____
4. Er ist auf der Flucht. _____

DI Blackwater meets Philipp Jackson the next morning back in Glasgow. The fat man is almost crying.
"Everything was an accident!" he says again.
"Rubbish. You posted aggressive comments online and made a death threat on live television," the inspector says.
"I don't remember making the call. I was drunk… It was only mind games! I just hated seeing Hunter all day, at

work and at home. And that silly song! It's so unfair that it's such a media success."

"I don't believe you. Now, what happened in the studio?"

"I wanted Hunter to fall. Yes, I put some oil on the ladder. But I didn't know that the inflatable cushion had a hole in it!"

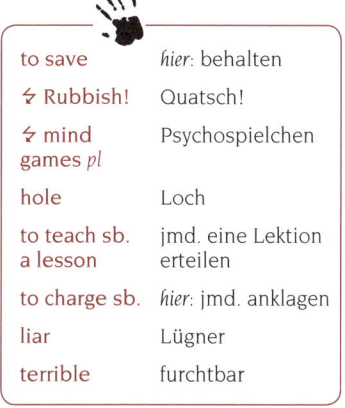

to save	*hier*: behalten
⚡ Rubbish!	Quatsch!
⚡ mind games *pl*	Psychospielchen
hole	Loch
to teach sb. a lesson	jmd. eine Lektion erteilen
to charge sb.	*hier*: jmd. anklagen
liar	Lügner
terrible	furchtbar

The inspector shakes her head. "Mr Jackson, you also threw a petrol bomb at Roy Hunter's car. I was there when it exploded. Was that an accident, too?"

"Yes, of course! I didn't want to hurt anyone. I only wanted to teach him a lesson!"

"And Aberdeen? Your ferry ticket?"

"I panicked. I thought Hunter was dead, so I ran away."

"Mr Jackson, I know when I'm hearing lies. I'm going to charge you later this morning. The discussions can wait."

"But Hunter's the liar, not me! Just ask him what he's really doing with the money from that terrible song…"

"Don't worry, I will," DI Blackwater tells him.

Final Test

Exercise 1: Odd one out. Welches Wort ist das schwarze Schaf? Unterstreichen Sie!

1. Catsbells   Keswick   Carlisle   Grasmere
2. startled   beautiful   excited   answered
3. DI   DNA   DS   WPC
4. hiking   studying   sailing   camping

Exercise 2: Verbs forms. Wie lautet das Present Simple und Past Simple der folgenden Verben in der dritten Person?

1. to go   _____   _____
2. to try   _____   _____
3. to buy   _____   _____
4. to throw   _____   _____
5. to watch   _____   _____
6. to catch   _____   _____
7. to eat   _____   _____
8. to drink   _____   _____

Exercise 3: Multiple choice. Welcher Satz ist korrekt? Kreuzen Sie an!

1. a) ❐ When I saw Rosie, she was alive and well.
   b) ❐ When I saw Rosie, she was alive and good.

2. a) ❐ Derwentwater is beautiful and quite.
   b) ❐ Derwentwater is beautiful and quiet.

3. a) ❐ I am looking forward to seeing you.
   b) ❐ I am looking forward to see you.

4. a) ❐ Is there any news about Dean?
   b) ❐ Are there any news about Dean?

5. a) ❐ I'm not sure. It doesn't give sense.
   b) ❐ I'm not sure. It doesn't make sense.

Exercise 4: Unscramble the words. Bringen Sie die Buchstaben in die richtige Reihenfolge!

1. Annabelle's car is a enrspet _____ from her father.
2. Martin is a marabn _____ at the Loft Nightclub.
3. Simon and Wendy are on dohayli _____.
4. McKenzie and Atkinson loves _____ the case.
5. Dean is a scuptse _____.

102

Exercise 5: Crossword puzzle. Lösen Sie das Kreuzworträtsel, indem Sie das deutsche Wort ins Englische übersetzen oder das fehlende Wort ergänzen!

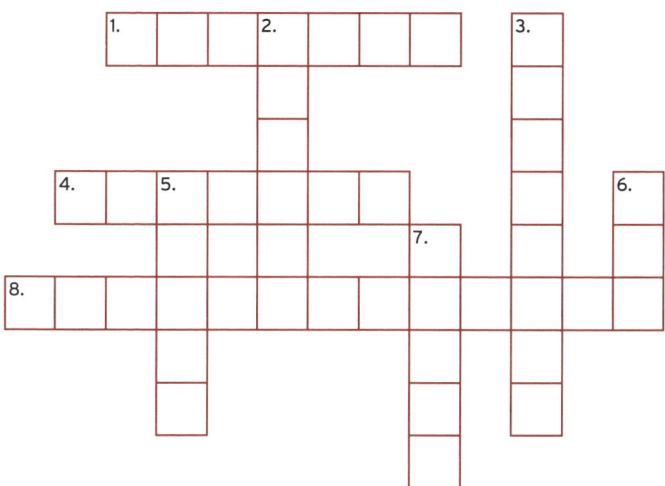

Across

1. The police **endlich** found the man three days later.
4. I fired him because he was **nichtsnutzig**.
8. Fortunately it was not a very long **Ermittlung**.

Down

2. An officer entered the pub to **verhaften** the man.
3. Derwentwater is in the Lake ...
5. **Jeder** evening he drinks half a bottle of whisky.
6. The killer left Glasgow and was on the ... .
7. The inspector was unable to **fangen** him.

Exercise 6: Unscramble. Bilden Sie Sätze aus den Wörtern!

1. Rosie's   was   accident   death   an

   _____

2. not   footballers   good   the   are   singers

   _____

3. the   drive   car   on   exploded   the   new

   _____

4. Blackwater   with   lives   in   two   her   sons   Glasgow

   _____

Exercise 7: Translation. Übersetzen Sie die Sätze ins Englische!

1. Ich wohne hier im Dorf.

   _____

2. Meine Mutter arbeitet in einem Laden.

   _____

3. Geht es dir gut? Deine Hände zittern.

   _____

4. Ich habe sein Fahrrad auf der Klippe gesehen.

   _____

Answers

A Cry in the Darkness

Exercise 1: 1. false (The air is cold.) 2. true 3. true 4. false (He's always up to no good.) 5. false (There is a fence at the cliff edge.)

Exercise 2: 1. on 2. is standing 3. are taking 4. are 5. cliff

Exercise 3: 1. d 2. e 3. b 4. a 5. c

Exercise 4: 1. at 2. to 3. down 4. between 5. in 6. on 7. of

Exercise 5: 1. washing 2. hose 3. to complain 4. gossip

Exercise 6:

							1.B		
		2.H	O	R	R	I	3.B	L	4.E
		U		E			Y		V
		S		A					I
		B		D					D
		A				5.H	O	S	E
6.P	O	I	N	T	S				N
		D							C
						7.C	A	S	E

Exercise 7: 1. runing (running) 2. all ready (already) 3. proffessor (professor) 4. stepps (steps) 5. angryly (angrily) 6. there (their)

Exercise 8: 1. village 2. update 3. murder 4. to stare at
Exercise 9: 1. facts 2. car 3. July 4. buses 5. taxi 6. alcohol
Exercise 10: 1. to buy 2. expensive 3. late 4. the least
Exercise 11: 1. disappear 2. honest 3. accident 4. remain silent 5. sweat 6. nail varnish
Hidden word: animals

Death at the Lake

Exercise 1: 1. boat 2. lake 3. sun 4. side 5. water
Exercise 2: 1. daughter 2. boyfriend 3. boss 4. wife
Exercise 3: 1. d 2. c 3. a 4. b
Exercise 4: 1. c 2. d 3. a 4. b
Exercise 5: 1. false (Atkinson knows where Dean lives.) 2. true 3. false (She finds Rosie's rucksack.) 4. false (Rosie left alone.)
Exercise 6: 1. at 2. in 3. on 4. in 5. on
Exercise 7: 1. excited 2. dead 3. sad 4. ancient
Exercise 8: 1. c 2. a 3. d 4. b
Exercise 9: **Across:** INVESTIGATE, SAMPLE, FORENSIC, CRIME, FINGERPRINT
Down: CLUE, DNA, SUSPECT
Exercise 10: 1. Its (It's) 2. hear (here) 3. Deans (Dean's) 4. anyone (someone) 5. off (of) 6. somethink (something)
Exercise 11: 1. b 2. d 3. a 4. c
Exercise 12: 1. false (Annabelle did it.) 2. false (Rosie was on her bicycle.) 3. true 4. true

Exercise 13: 1. notices, noticed 2. is, was 3. solves, solved 4. says, said 5. has, had 6. cries, cried

Deadly Duet

Exercise 1: 1. true 2. false (They are not good friends.) 3. true 4. false (They have no musical talent.)

Exercise 2: 1. name 2. young 3. What's 4. Who's 5. hand 6. boy

Exercise 3: 1. already 2. silly 3. striker 4. generous 5. viewer(s) 6. island 7. annoying 8. voice

Exercise 4: 1. is analysing 2. has 3. is 4. take 5. wants

Exercise 5: 1. lie 2. contract 3. embarrass 4. reply 5. heavily 6. seriously 7. agree 8. yawn
Hidden word: interview

Exercise 6: 1. planks 2. water 3. early 4. legs 5. audience

Exercise 7: 1. c 2. d 3. a 4. b

Exercise 8: 1. cushion 2. ball 3. to yawn 4. silly

Exercise 9: 1. inspektor (inspector) 2. extremly (extremely) 3. peeple (people) 4. your (you're) 5. thinks (things) 6. every thing (everything)

Exercise 10: 1. window 2. moment 3. fire 4. friend

Exercise 11: 1. b 2. c 3. d 4. a

Exercise 12: 1. on 2. in 3. up 4. on 5. in 6. by

Exercise 13: 1. slowly 2. to pause/to stop 3. to act 4. useless 5. to remember 6. start

Exercise 14: 1. Last orders! 2. Shut up! 3. Hands off! 4. He's on the run.

Final Test

Exercise 1: **1.** Carlisle **2.** answered **3.** DNA **4.** studying

Exercise 2: **1.** goes, went **2.** tries, tried **3.** buys, bought **4.** throws, threw **5.** watches, watched **6.** catches, caught **7.** eats, ate **8.** drinks, drank

Exercise 3: **1.** a **2.** b **3.** a **4.** a **5.** b

Exercise 4: **1.** present **2.** barman **3.** holiday **4.** solve **5.** suspect

Exercise 5:

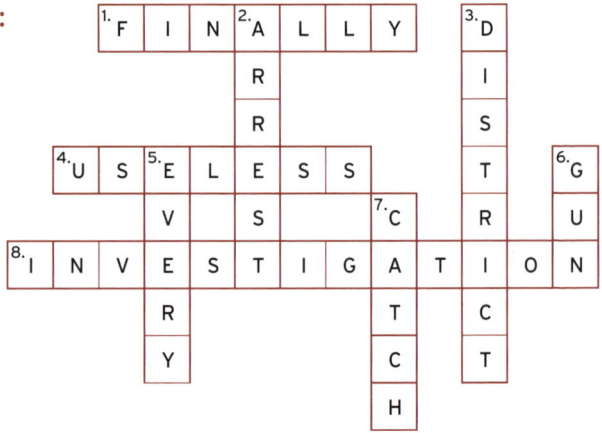

Exercise 6:
1. Rosie's death was an accident.
2. The footballers are not good singers.
3. The new car exploded on the drive.
4. Blackwater lives in Glasgow with her two sons.

Exercise 7:
1. I live here in the village.
2. My mother works in a shop.
3. Are you okay? Your hands are shaking.
4. I saw his bike on the cliff.

Glossary

⚡ = umgangssprachlich
pl = Plural

about	*hier*: circa
to absorb	aufnehmen
accident	Unfall
to act	eingreifen, handeln
to add	ergänzen
⚡ ages ago	vor einer Ewigkeit
ago	vor
to agree	zustimmen
to argue	sich streiten
almost	fast
already	schon, bereits
ambulance	Krankenwagen
ancient	sehr alt
animal rights activist	Tierschützer(in)
annoying	lästig
anyway	jedenfalls
to arrest	festnehmen
as... as...	so ... wie ...

at once	sofort
audience	Publikum
autograph	Autogramm
back-stabbing	hinterhältig
backwards	rückwärts
bark	Gebell
beer can	Bierdose
to be (was, been) in a hurry	es eilig haben
to be (was, been) supposed to	sollen
⚡ to be (was, been) up to no good	nichts Gutes im Schilde führen
to believe	glauben
to bend (bent, bent) down	sich bücken
body	*hier*: Leiche
bonfire	(Lager-)Feuer
boot	*hier*: Kofferraum
to breathe out heavily	tief ausatmen
broken	kaputt, (ab)gebrochen
building	Gebäude
to burn (burnt, burnt)	(ver)brennen
by	*hier*: bis
capital	*hier*: Hauptstadt
careful(ly)	vorsichtig
case	*hier*: Fall
to catch (caught, caught)	fangen
to cause	verursachen

CCTV camera	Überwachungskamera
certainly	sicher(lich)
chain	Kette
challenge	Wettbewerb
to charge sb.	*hier*: jmd. anklagen
cheeky	frech
to cheer	jubeln
chest	Brust
cliff	Klippe
closing time	Sperrstunde
clue	Hinweis
coincidence	Zufall
to come in for questioning	zur Vernehmung erscheinen
commercial break	Werbepause
to complain	(sich be)klagen
concerned	besorgt
to confirm	bestätigen
confused	verwirrt
contract	Vertrag
to count oneself lucky	sich glücklich schätzen
couple	Paar
crate	Kiste
crime	Verbrechen
crime scene	Tatort
crowded	überfüllt
cry	Schrei
to cry (out)	schreien, ausrufen
curly	lockig

customer	Kunde
cut	Schnitt(wunde)
damaged	beschädigt
⚡ Damn!	Verdammt!
death threat	Morddrohung
dental records *pl*	Zahnarztunterlagen
desk	Schreibtisch
Detective Chief Inspector (DCI)	Hauptkommissar(in)
Detective Inspector (DI)	Kriminalkommissarin(in)
Detective Sergeant (DS)	Kriminalmeister(in)
diary	Tagebuch
to disappear	verschwinden
disgusting	ekelhaft
to disturb	stören
doorway	Eingangstür
drive	*hier*: Auffahrt
driving licence	Führerschein
drunk	betrunken
dustbin	Mülltonne
either	*hier*: auch nicht
elderly	ältere(r, s)
to embarrass	blamieren
evidence	Hinweise, Beweis(e)
to examine	untersuchen
excited	aufgeregt
to feel (felt, felt) sick	einem ist übel
fence	Zaun
ferry	Fähre

to fetch	holen
finally	endlich
fingerprint	Fingerabdruck
fire engine	Feuerwehrauto
to fire sb.	jmd. feuern
to flash	blinken
flat	Wohnung
flatmate	Mitbewohner(in)
folded across one's chest	vor der Brust verschränkt
foolish	töricht
for charity	für einen guten Zweck
frightened	verängstigt
to frown	die Stirn runzeln
gasp	hörbares Einatmen
to gasp	keuchen
generous	großzügig
gesture	Geste
to get (got, got) rid of sth.	etw. loswerden
glasses *pl*	Brille
glove	Handschuh
to go (went, gone) off	*hier*: losgehen
gossip	Klatsch
hall	Diele
handcuffs *pl*	Handschellen
handlebar	Fahrradlenker
Hands off!	Finger weg!
to hang (hung, hung) on	warten
to hang (hung, hung) up	*hier*: auflegen

to hate	hassen
to have (had, had) an argument	sich streiten
to have (had, had) no idea	keine Ahnung haben
hedge	Hecke
hedge cuttings *pl*	Heckenabschnitt
to hide (hid, hidden)	verbergen, verstecken
to hire	mieten
hit	*hier*: Klick
to hit (hit, hit) sb.	jmd. schlagen; mit jmd. zusammenstoßen
to hit (hit, hit) the bull's eye	ins Schwarze treffen
hole	Loch
honest	ehrlich
horrible	abscheulich
hose	Schlauch
hothead	Hitzkopf
to hurry	sich beeilen
to hurt (hurt, hurt) sb.	jmd. verletzen
husband	Ehemann
ID card	Ausweis
identification	Ausweispapiere
I'm afraid so.	Ich fürchte ja.
imagination	Vorstellungskraft
impatiently	ungeduldig
impossible	unmöglich
including	inklusive

inflatable cushion	aufblasbare Matte
innocent	unschuldig
instead	stattdessen
to interrupt	unterbrechen
to investigate	ermitteln
investigation	Ermittlung
island	Insel
journey	Reise
to kneel (knelt, knelt) down	sich hinknien
lab (laboratory)	Labor
lad	Kerl
ladder	Leiter
last orders *pl*	letzte Runde
lazy	faul
to lend (lent, lent) sb. sth.	jmd. etw. ausleihen
liar	Lügner(in)
lie	Lüge
lively	belebt
local	einheimisch
locals *pl*	Einheimische
to look forward to	sich auf etw. freuen
to look into	untersuchen
lost and found office	Fundbüro
loud	*hier*: grell
lovely	herrlich
lovers' lane	lauschiges, romantisches Plätzchen

to make (made, made) sense	Sinn ergeben
manslaughter	fahrlässige Tötung
map	Landkarte
mark	Fleck, Schramme
meanwhile	in der Zwischenzeit
⚡ mind games *pl*	Psychospielchen
missing	*hier*: verschwunden, vermisst
moody	launisch
movement	Bewegung
Ms	Frau (Anrede)
mugging	Überfall (auf offener Straße)
murder	Mord
to mutter	murmeln
mystery	*hier*: geheimnisumwoben
nail varnish	Nagellack
narrow	eng
to nod	nicken
noise	Geräusch
to notice	bemerken
obstacle course	Hindernislauf
Oh dear!	Oh je!
on the run	auf der Flucht
opposite	gegenüber
out of breath	außer Atem
to overtake (-took, -taken)	überholen
to panic	in Panik geraten
past	*hier*: vorbei (an)

path	Pfad
to pay sb. back	es jmd. heimzahlen
phone records *pl*	Telefonverbindungsdaten
pie	Pastete
pile	Stapel
to point (at)	zeigen (auf), zielen (auf)
Police Constable (PC)	Polizist(in)
prank call	Telefonstreich
pregnant	schwanger
to prepare	vorbereiten
presenter	Moderator(in)
probably	wahrscheinlich
producer	Produzent(in)
to protect	schützen
proud	stolz
purse	Geldbeutel, Portemonnaie
to put out an APB (all points bulletin)	zur Fahndung ausschreiben
quite	ziemlich
to raise	hochziehen
to reach	erreichen
recent	neu, aus jüngster Zeit
recordings *pl*	(Video-)Aufnahmen
referee	Schiedsrichter(in)
to regret	bereuen
regular	Stammkunde/-kundin
rehearsal	Probe
relationship	Beziehung
to remain silent	schweigen

to remember	sich erinnern
to rent	mieten
to repeat	wiederholen
to reply	antworten
to report	berichten
responsible	verantwortlich
retired	in Rente
right away	sofort
ring tone	Klingelton
rivals *pl*	Gegner
to rob sb.	jmd. ausrauben
rubbish	Abfälle
⚡ Rubbish!	Quatsch!
rude word	Schimpfwort
safe	sicher
to sail	segeln
sample	Probe
to save	*hier*: behalten
sb.'s ears are ringing	jmd. klingen die Ohren
scared	verängstigt
scarf	Schal
scholarship	Stipendium
scratch	Kratzer
screen	Bildschirm
screenshot	Bildschirmfoto
⚡ scum	Abschaum
search warrant	Durchsuchungsbefehl
security camera footage	Sicherheitskameraaufnahmen

to see (saw, seen) the point	den Sinn verstehen
serious(ly)	ernst
set	*hier*: Fernsehbühne
several	mehrere
to shake (shook, shaken)	zittern
to shake one's head	den Kopf schütteln
shaken	*hier*: erschüttert
shaky	zittrig
sharply	*hier*: kritisch, aufmerksam
shed	Schuppen
sheet	Laken
shelf (*pl*: shelves)	Regal
to shine (shone, shone) a torch	mit einer Taschenlampe leuchten
short	*hier*: klein
shouting	Geschrei
⚡ Shut up!	Halt die Klappe!
sign	Zeichen
silly	albern
sink	Spülbecken
size	Größe
smash hit	Superhit
to solve	lösen
to spend (spent, spent)	ausgeben; verbringen
spot	*hier*: Ort
to squeal	kreischen, quieken
to stammer	stottern
to stare at (sb.)	(jmd.) anstarren

startled	erschrocken
step	Schritt
strange	seltsam
stretching exercise	Dehnübung
striker	Stürmer(in)
struggle	Kampf
suddenly	plötzlich
to succeed	Erfolg haben, erfolgreich sein
suicide	Selbstmord
sunglasses *pl*	Sonnenbrille
suspect	Verdächtige(r)
suspicious	verdächtig
to sweat	schwitzen
to take (took, taken) sb.'s place	an jds. Stelle treten
to teach (taught, taught) sb. a lesson	jmd. eine Lektion erteilen
to tell (told, told) the truth	die Wahrheit sagen
tent	Zelt
terrible	furchtbar
that reminds me…	wobei mir einfällt …
to thump	(mit der Faust) schlagen
tie	Krawatte
to tie	(fest)binden
to tie one's laces	sich die Schnürsenkel binden
tight	*hier*: fest
timber-framed	Fachwerk…
topless bar	Oben-ohne-Bar

torch	Taschenlampe
trigger	Auslöser, Abzug
trouble	Problem(e), Schwierigkeiten
useless	nichtsnutzig
view	Ausblick, Aussicht
viewers *pl*	Zuschauer
voice	Stimme
voice recorder	Diktiergerät
What's going on?	Was ist los?
What took you so long?	Wo sind Sie so lange geblieben?
to whisper	flüstern
wife	Ehefrau
to wipe	wischen, abtrocknen
woods	Wäldchen
WPC (Woman Police Constable)	Polizistin
to yawn	gähnen
You are under arrest.	Sie sind verhaftet.
zip line	Seilrutsche

List of Exercises

	Focus	Exercise	Page
A Cry in the Darkness			
1	Comprehension	True or false?	8
2	Grammar	Choose the correct alternative	9
3	Vocabulary	Match up the words	11
4	Grammar	Prepositions	14
5	Vocabulary	Odd one out	17
6	Vocabulary	Crossword puzzle	19
7	Vocabulary	Spelling mistakes	22
8	Vocabulary	Definitions	24
9	Vocabulary	Fill in the blanks	26
10	Vocabulary	Opposites	29
11	Vocabulary	Translation quiz	34
Death at the Lake			
1	Vocabulary	Missing words	37
2	Comprehension	Relationship matching	40
3	Comprehension	Unscramble the text	42
4	Vocabulary	Translating adjectives	45
5	Comprehension	True or false?	47
6	Grammar	Prepositions	49
7	Vocabulary	Opposites	53
8	Vocabulary	Match up the phrases	55
9	Vocabulary	Police work quiz	56
10	Grammar	Correct the mistakes	60
11	Vocabulary	Definitions	62
12	Comprehension	True or false?	65
13	Grammar	Verb forms	66

	Focus	Exercise	Page
Deadly Duet			
1	Comprehension	True or false?	69
2	Vocabulary	Fill in the blanks	71
3	Vocabulary	Word search	73
4	Grammar	Choose the correct alternative	77
5	Vocabulary	Translation quiz	79
6	Vocabulary	Unscramble	81
7	Vocabulary	Match up the words	84
8	Vocabulary	Odd one out	85
9	Vocabulary	Spelling mistakes	87
10	Vocabulary	Definitions	90
11	Vocabulary	Phrasal verbs	91
12	Grammar	Prepositions	94
13	Vocabulary	Opposites	96
14	Vocabulary	Idioms	98
Final Test			
1	Vocabulary	Odd one out	101
2	Grammar	Verb forms	101
3	Grammar	Multiple choice	102
4	Vocabulary	Unscramble the words	102
5	Vocabulary	Crossword puzzle	103
6	Grammar	Unscramble	104
7	Vocabulary	Translation	104

Notizen

Sprachtraining Englisch
Übung macht den Meister!

144 Seiten
ISBN 978-3-8174-1648-6

Das Übungsbuch ist ideal für Anfänger und Wiedereinsteiger, die ihre Englischkenntnisse auffrischen und vertiefen möchten. Rund 200 thematisch sortierte Übungen zu Wortschatz und Grammatik machen das Training abwechslungsreich und effektiv.

Infokästen erklären sprachliche und landeskundliche Besonderheiten. Lösungen und Glossar im Anhang.

Extra: Krimilektüre für Anfänger – so wird das Sprachtraining noch spannender!

Auch für Niveau A2-B1 erhältlich:
144 Seiten
ISBN 978-3-8174-1764-3

Spannend Sprachen lernen

Kriminell gut

ISBN 978-3-8174-2147-3

Lernlektüre für geübte Anfänger

- fesselnder Krimi von muttersprachlichem Autor
- über 50 didaktisch geprüfte Übungen
- Vokabelangaben auf jeder Seite und umfangreiches Glossar
- Infokästen zu Land und Sprache
- Online-Vokabeltraining mit phase6

Anonyme Drohbriefe und eine Explosion in einem Vorort von Manchester. Wurde die lokale Abgeordnete Opfer eines Anschlags? Inspector Hudson nimmt die Ermittlungen auf, die nicht nur politische Verstrickungen enthüllen, sondern auch ins Drogenmilieu von Manchester führen …
Hochspannung auf Englisch!

www.circonverlag.de

Unterhaltsam und spannend Sprachen lernen

Abwechslungsreiche Lektüren von Krimi bis Kurzgeschichten

- in über zehn Sprachen
- mit über 150 Titeln
- verfasst von Muttersprachlern
- von ganz leicht bis anspruchsvoll

Hier können Sie das aktuelle Verlagsprogramm einsehen und Ihren Wunschtitel gleich online bestellen:

www.circonverlag.de

circon